LETTERS FROM LOCKDOWN

Letters from Lockdown

A Selection of Covid C...
BBC Radio 4's PM ...

Duckworth & Worford
LONDON

Letters from Lockdown

A Selection of Covid Chronicles from
BBC Radio 4's *PM* Programme

Chatto & Windus
LONDON

1 3 5 7 9 10 8 6 4 2

Chatto & Windus, an imprint of Vintage

Chatto & Windus is part of the Penguin Random House
group of companies whose addresses can be found at
global.penguinrandomhouse.com

Foreword Copyright © BBC 2020

The moral right of Evan Davis as author of the foreword has been
asserted in accordance with the Copyright, Designs and Patents Act 1988

The BBC logo is a trademark of the British Broadcasting Corporation and
is used under licence BBC logo © BBC 1996 Radio 4 logo © BBC 2008

£1 from the price of this book will benefit BBC Children in Need
(registered charity number 802052 in England & Wales and SC039557 in
Scotland)

First published by Chatto & Windus in 2020

penguin.co.uk/vintage

A CIP catalogue record for this book is available from
the British Library

'In the Dark Times', originally published in German in 1939 as 'Motto: In
den finsteren Zeiten', translated by Tom Kuhn. Copyright © 1976, 1961
by Bertolt-Brecht-Erben / Suhrkamp Verlag, from *Collected Poems of Bertolt
Brecht* by Bertolt Brecht, translated by Tom Kuhn and David Constantine.
Used by permission of Liveright Publishing Corporation.

ISBN 9781784744342

Typeset in 11/15 pt Baskerville BT
by Integra Software Services Pvt. Ltd, Pondicherry

Printed and bound in Great Britain by Clays Ltd, Elcograf S.p.A.

Penguin Random House is committed to a sustainable future for our
business, our readers and our planet. This book is made from Forest
Stewardship Council® certified paper.

In the dark times
Will there also be singing?
Yes, there will also be singing.
About the dark times.

Bertolt Brecht

Contents

Foreword

Evan Davis

Presenter of BBC Radio 4's PM

It was extraordinary how quickly Covid-19 caught up with us.

For much of January 2020, it was just another news story from a distant place in the lower reaches of the *PM* programme's running order. As a foreign disaster, it was competing with the Australian bushfires for our attention; our eyes were squarely focused on Brexit, scheduled for 31 January. I had spent much of 2018 and 2019 boldly asserting to colleagues and friends that the national ordeal of debating how we'd leave the EU would be the biggest thing to happen to our country in our lifetimes, and that we could look forward to 2020 as the year during which things might calm down a bit.

But coronavirus-related events moved rapidly. By 11 February, when the World Health Organisation first gave the disease its name, it was a daily headline. And soon the virus was jumping continents: by the time it landed in northern Italy, it was the only story anyone was talking about. All of a sudden, it felt ominously close to home. A colleague returned from Milan, where he'd taken a weekend trip to see the Inter Milan-Sampdoria football match on 24 February. The match was postponed on account of Covid-19, but when he got back if we so much as heard him clear his throat in the office we couldn't help but think: 'Has he brought it here?' (He hadn't.)

Soon after, I remember the *PM* editor began to attend BBC management meetings planning for a Covid-19 contingency. 'It might mean operating with a quarter of staff absent,' she told me.

Of course, everything we thought back then seems incredibly naïve now. We had no idea what was about to hit us. In early March I think it dawned on us how serious the situation was becoming. Soon we stopped asking 'what's so special about Italy that it has suffered it so badly?' and quickly moved to 'could Britain have it as bad as Italy?' and before long the question became 'why has the UK had it so much worse?'

Never before have such complacent assumptions and casual misunderstandings been so abruptly overturned.

Once we entered the most serious phase from late March to May, at *PM* – in common with journalists everywhere – we were very aware that history was being made. This was no ordinary story: it was not just the magnitude of the implications of the disease, nor the fact that virtually none of our listeners had ever lived through anything like it. It was that in contrast to most of our running news stories, this one affected the lives of everyone in a very dramatic way. Including ourselves and our own families.

And we quickly realised that aside from all the daily news angles to be covered – the disease itself, the deaths, the effect on hospitals, care homes and schools, the science, the politics – this was above all a shared national experience. It was a phenomenon that aroused common sentiments – bewilderment and fear, concern and uncertainty, as well as a sense of neighbourliness and solidarity. Yet it was also a period in which every family had their own private story – their own challenges, hopes and fears.

In order to reflect the full range of ways in which Covid-19 affected everyday life we needed members of the public to contribute their stories.

Given the speed of events, we barely gave any thought to the name of the slot we were creating – Covid Chronicles seemed to fit the bill – and we simply suggested listeners may like to make a contribution of about 400 words, with the plan to have some of the submissions read on air.

The response exceeded our wildest expectations: in quantity, in quality and in their sheer variety. We were delighted with the submissions. They brilliantly reflected the feeling of a shared challenge – of a nation day by day making sense of an unfathomable year. And they opened our eyes to the drastically different ways Covid-19 affected different people up and down the country.

Our first on-air Covid Chronicle laid out the experience of a woman giving birth at the height of the crisis. It was just one moving example of an ordinary person writing the history of the pandemic as they lived through it. We soon had entries from adults young and old; from those who had lost someone, to those tending the sick or who were sick themselves; we had submissions from children and pieces about pets; we had entries from all corners of the United Kingdom, and even some from beyond its shores.

For me, the Chronicles were particularly important in balancing our coverage towards the personal rather than the political. For many of the keenest consumers of daily news programmes, politics is the main pre-occupation – and in the wake of Brexit, passions were inflamed and divisions intense. Certainly, the handling of the pandemic – reflected in the daily Downing Street briefings – was an important part of the story, and it was not hard to find people angry at the failings of the authorities to deal quickly and effectively with Covid-19. But there is a temptation in the news industry to frame all reporting that way – to think of every development as important primarily in providing a commentary on the performance of our elected leaders. But the Chronicles indicated that many people were not viewing their experience through that lens. This was a huge event, and they were not looking to it as an excuse for an argument; they just had plenty to think about in their own lives.

The Covid Chronicles added a human dimension to our coverage. What also became abundantly clear was that many listeners found it clarifying or even therapeutic to note down their feelings and to create something out of the wreckage. And during lockdown people of course had much more time than usual at home. What better way to use it than to become a modern-day Samuel Pepys and to contribute to the people's history of the pandemic?

This volume only contains a fraction of the thousands of Chronicles that have been written during the pandemic. Choosing a selection for publication is inevitably a difficult task, but we have been grateful for every one of the Chronicles that have been submitted, which I feel provide a testament to the resilience of ordinary people when confronted with the most exceptional circumstances.

LOCKDOWN

Xavier

Self Isle-Solation

30 March 2020

Summer seems to arrive sooner in the Western Isles than it does in other parts of the UK. Though chilly winds still whistle the tune of the long winter that has just passed, lambs bleat, peewits call to each other with both the sound and exhilaration of a dog that has just been given a new squeaky toy, and passing geese give honks of celebration over the Machair as the islands bask in an unprecedented forty-eight hours without rain. The sun has finally come out. In a few weeks' time, there won't be many places in the world as beautiful as this. As far as self-isolation is concerned, there's no place better suited. There are no confirmed cases of Covid-19 here in South Uist yet and, in some ways, not that much has changed. The schools may be off, the pubs closed and the ferries passengerless, but with so much island space to be shared out amongst such a finite number of people, there is almost no chance of a walk to the beach causing you to come into contact with someone from outside your own family bubble. The island has never buzzed with the potentially dangerous human interaction that is so apparent in epicentres like London. However, it still seems incredible that a place – where shops and medical centres come under immense strain after just a couple of days of bad weather – can remain so apparently unfazed by the greatest peace-time crisis the country has seen for over 100 years.

We are used to being kept inside by torrential wind and rain. We are used to being separated from the rest of society. We are used to coming together as a community to look after each other. However, the sense of community here means that when tragedy strikes the whole island feels it. So far, Covid has not struck and maybe this is why it doesn't quite seem real to everyone – why crofters who are well into their eighties are still needing to be told that they must stay at home. Today, Orkney confirmed its first case of the virus. The Western Isles is now the only UK health board without one. Of the 1,000 patients registered at the medical practice here, a third are in the vulnerable group – a third of the island's community potentially at risk. The birds may be singing and the sun finally shining, but here on South Uist, we wait with bated breath.

Clare
Mothering Sunday

11 June 2020

It is Mothering Sunday, 22 March 2020. I am sitting in my living room, staring at my computer screen. It is a Sunday when we are supposed to celebrate and give thanks for our own mothers. We take this seriously in our family. I have bought a card that says, 'Mothering Sunday' rather than 'Mother's Day' and truly see it as a celebration of mothering and motherhood. My mother is 300 miles away. I last saw her a month ago – just four months after my dad died. She is on her own this year, although we are able to help her navigate Zoom – the new tool which is slowly becoming a prominent part of our lives, a poor substitute for a shared meal and a hug.

It is Mothering Sunday, 22 March 2020. I sit in my garden on this sunny morning. My husband says Mass for what will be the last time, in an empty church. It is a Sunday when we are supposed to celebrate and give thanks for the Church as our mother. We also give thanks for Mary, the mother of Jesus, and here in this place, this is such a natural part of the rhythm of prayer and worship. And yet here I am, drawing flowers and blowing bubbles on a picnic rug, in a feeble attempt to connect with God and St Mary's church itself, which is next door to my house.

It is Mothering Sunday, 22 March 2020. I am delivering flowers to women who are self-isolating and will not see their children today, or in some cases, anyone. It is a Sunday when we are supposed to celebrate and give thanks for all forms of mothering. Some of the women we will see today are mothers, some of them are nuns, some of them are elderly widows and some are single. We knock on each door, leave a posy on the doorstep and then stand well back. At each house we are greeted with a smile and heartfelt thanks. At one, the lady in question pops her head out of the attic window – in fear of the virus, she is even isolating from her own husband.

It is Mothering Sunday, 22 March 2020. I am in pain. It is a Sunday when we are supposed to celebrate and give thanks for motherhood. Three days previous I was told that there was no heart-beat and that I would miscarry naturally. For eight weeks I have been a mother and now there is no longer anything to celebrate or give thanks for. I have to enter the hospital alone to confirm that all that was, has passed. The woman who touches and checks me will come closer to me than any other human – other than my husband – for the next twelve weeks. Tomorrow, we go into lockdown.

Felicity

Sick With the Virus

30 March 2020

You're sick. And you're still sick. But now you're no longer so weak that you can't occasionally leave the bedroom, that silent room with the blue outside, far, far away. You're in this strange painful dance with the one you love who cares for you, who's cared for you for days.

You put the glass and coffee cup there on the kitchen surface. Then bundle yourself away, trying to stretch two metres away from them. You're in the bathroom already now, hiding out. Don't touch anything. They enter, stage right. Pour water in the glass for your tired throat. They refill your cup, with coffee you haven't smelled or tasted for a week. You love that they make coffee for you. They joke how you always want coffee on a drip. The coffee is now cold. You both know it would be better hot. You can taste the heat.

They open the microwave. You watch from the bathroom. They retreat out of the kitchen. You advance. Fetch the cup and put it in the microwave. Back in the bathroom. They return, close the door, heat the coffee, open the microwave door, an invitation. Leave. You walk forward, look at the steaming coffee. Fantasise about its taste and smell as the cup sits miserable in the ugly microwave. Remember three weeks ago when you made coffee to take with you to the cold picket line. Life has been strange for a long time. Grab the cup. Walk through the kitchen. Pick up the water glass too. They are pushed against the wall in the living room. Keeping distance from you as they must. You pass them. You're back in the bedroom. No one has touched the wrong thing. The coffee's been made hot by many hands. None touching. You drink it alone.

Do these apotropaic gestures work? Work to keep the sickness away from them. To carve new lines in your home. To make relations with objects. They're already a way of life. And they are not sick, yet. If they fall sick you will make them tea. They fell out of love with coffee. You know they are afraid of falling sick. As you were.

In the silent room you drink the coffee they made for you. You dream how you will tend to them, try to make them feel safe. One day, touch will return.

Nik
A Final Touch

30 March 2020

I'm sitting in a patient's room and through the window I can see the well-maintained garden lit by the sharp, crisp spring sunlight. The sky is clear of aeroplanes and the roads free of the usual everyday traffic – both conspicuous in their absence. I'm sitting holding the hand of a patient who is dying. They appear so peaceful and the birdsong is so carefree it almost feels beautiful. This moment stands out in my mind because the spread of Covid-19 means this will possibly be the last time I hold someone's hand at work without gloves or a mask on. As such I'm more aware of feelings that perhaps I had come to take for granted – the warmth of my hand versus the coolness of theirs, the colour of my skin compared to theirs, the sound of my own breathing compared to their gentle breaths.

Caring for someone at the end of life is a privilege and I feel that now more than ever. I am

11

also aware of how lucky I am to have this work and how fortunate it makes me – and my wife, who also works for the NHS as a GP. Although we know that going to work puts us at risk, we have each other when we are home and we, unlike many, are not having to worry about paying bills. We were due to start IVF in the hopes of expanding our family but that dream must be put on hold for now – a small price to pay compared to most. Taking time to consider what I am thankful for is proving to be a very positive way to start each day.

I hope that in the coming days, weeks, months, that the people I meet at work will still be able to sense that beneath the apron, the gloves and the mask, I'm still a person, like them. I hope that I can convey my feelings to them not just through the words that come muffled through the protective equipment but also through the look in my eyes. So they will know that, like everyone else working in the NHS – be that in the emergency department, the hospital wards, the nursing homes or in the homes of our patients – we are there with them, we will take care of them and we aren't going anywhere.

Stephen

Closing the Church Doors

30 March 2020

When I closed and locked the doors of the church I knelt down in a pew and cried. People come here to pray, to give thanks, to share their fears and their joys. But now the House of God is locked up and there are to be no services there, and I wonder if God's mercy has also been closed to us. As the priest of this parish I feel as though I have abandoned my people in their time of need.

So I have taken lots of things down from church to the Vicarage; vestments and a chalice, books and bread and wine, and my dining room has become the parish church for the time being. From here I broadcast Morning Prayer and celebrate the Eucharist all by myself, uploading it online. I wonder if anyone is watching, and if any of it matters.

And then my parishioners send me photos of them standing and kneeling in front of laptops and smartphones. They write to me words of encouragement saying, 'I have just watched the Mass online . . . I really felt that I was almost there in church with you,' and another, 'It means a great deal to us to share in the services online. God bless everyone.'

A priest is many things. Sometimes we are social workers or event organisers, administrators and publicists, but the one completely unique thing we do is pray on behalf of the people, the parish and the world. Perhaps these lonely services will renew the sense that prayer is at the heart of who I am and what I do – and that when any of us prays, we are never alone because we are always invisibly joined to everyone else who is also praying, on earth and in heaven.

Holy Week and Easter is my favourite time of the year. Just when the beauty of spring is bursting forth, there are all the dramatic and beautiful liturgies, with stripping of altars and kissing of crosses, and lighting of fires at dawn, and then on Easter Day the church is filled with the intoxicating scent of lilies and daffodils. I can hardly bear the thought that we won't share in these things this year.

I often go into the church when I pass by on my daily exercise or on the way to the shops. I check that where we keep the Sacrament the candle is lit, bless the bread at the Eucharist and replace the candle when it runs low. I think of the day when I shall take the key and unlock the doors, and the people will come in again – and they will see that all along, the light was burning in the darkness. That God was there with us all the time. Then I know that although Easter will be later this year, it will come.

Kate

Return from Antarctica

March 2020

'It says here that you'll have to isolate yourself for three months when you get back,' said one of my fellow passengers.

'Oh yes,' I responded, rather casually.

I was aware of Covid-19, which was just emerging as I left for the Antarctic adventure that I had been looking forward to for over a year. All of us on our small boat, on our trip-of-a-lifetime, had had our temperatures checked on embarkation and no one had become ill since. Now, coming to the end of our cruise – fourteen days of isolation in the safest continent – the impending pandemic was sneaking up on those adventures with whales and penguins.

Then came the message from my third daughter that she thought she had the virus (only a mild dose, fortunately) and my heart joined up with my head. It WAS real.

We were informed that Argentina wouldn't let us dock in Ushuaia as scheduled, nor Buenos Aires. Uruguay, however, would give us three days in Montevideo, but we were not to book anything until we were actually there.

All plans changed.

Into this limbo of a bonus voyage along the Argentinian coast came a greater sense of solidarity and camaraderie. Already a cohesive and friendly group, drawn from all ages and walks of life, we were figuratively as well as literally all in the same boat. Passengers, staff and crew stepped up to the mark and arranged lectures, yoga classes, treasure hunts, games tournaments and quizzes. We had great fun, and the bar remained open.

Then came the time to rebook flights. When 100 people are simultaneously trying to use the ship's internet, it's not easy. 'Stay on the boat till it gets back to Holland,' said my second daughter, 'it's the safest place.'

Stress levels rose and passengers were constantly huddled over phones. Friends and family acted as booking agents. My first daughter liaised for me through WhatsApp and eventually I was

17

one of those who could shout, 'Got one!' and get the universal cheer. Everyone eventually managed a flight out.

We realised that this might be the last time we could hug for quite a long while, so it was World Hug Day for three days.

Passports were handed over to officials in buckets on ropes and, group by group, passengers departed on the coach that would take them, with motorcycle outriders and police escort, speeding through all the red lights to the airport in Montevideo. Remaining passengers cheered from the decks.

I was one of the last to leave and had to go the long way round, via Chile and Brazil, to get back to London. But I felt truly blessed. I was going home, I felt safe in a cradle of hugs, genuine friendship and family support, enough to see me through whatever was to come in the changed world I was about to enter, even if it did mean three months of lockdown.

Maya

Uni Life is Not the Same

03 July 2020

I'm woken one day by aggressive knocking on my bedroom door.

'Don't open the door,' shouts my housemate from the other side, when my suddenly-awake-panic indicates to her that I am conscious. 'I have coronavirus and we all have to self-isolate.'

What???

All but two of my housemates escaped Birmingham before lockdown could lock them down, yet the incubation period situation worries us all. The one with coronavirus had been showing symptoms for a week. Have any of us already picked up the virus from her? We start arguing in the group chat about whether or not to self-isolate. 'What's the point if we all have it already?', versus, 'We have to isolate just in case, let's not take any chances.'

On the second floor, the other remaining housemate starts coughing.

'STAY IN YOUR ROOM!' she capslocks at me over WhatsApp. 'YOU'RE AT RISK! YOU HAVE ASTHMA!'

Avoiding each other in the same house, our only communication has become through Whats-App. Being an introvert in a big university, I'm used to burning myself out on social interaction then hiding in my room. But by the fourth day of self-isolation, I was getting lonely.

Day 7, I'm wishing I was home. My parents had planned to pick me up on March 25th. Then Boris announced lockdown.

Day 12, we run into each other in the kitchen, and it's such a relief. After days of worry, and of trying to keep each other safe, the emotional effects of separation and reunion bonds us closer. We didn't last the full fourteen days, but the loneliness was becoming more of a threat than the virus itself. Being introverted doesn't give me isolation-coping superpowers.

The university emails us updates.

'Exams are cancelled!' exclaims a housemate in outrage, whose course is 80 per cent examination based. On top of that, work placements for second-year students like her have evaporated, leaving career plans in ruins. And it sucks for third-year students, who are abruptly graduating with neither final exams, ceremony, nor job opportunities.

Virtual classes makes uni life underwhelming. I could have taken courses remotely, instead of moving away to live with a bunch of strangers in an unfamiliar city. But that's what uni life is all about. It's about renting student accommodation with a group of new friends and being grown-up without most of the responsibilities. It's about being surrounded by people from all over the planet, feeling as though the whole world is around you.

Now that's gone. However, the bubbles we've retreated to aren't the worst. In this indefinitely extended holiday, my housemates are teaching me to cook. It doesn't feel so lonely when we're looking after each other.

Nishma

Untouched Dresses in the Drawer

03 April 2020

Her best dresses lie in the drawer untouched. It matters even less what she wears now: there is no one else to see.

The apocalyptic world has arrived unnoticed by my seven-month-old daughter. Her world view is still inhabited, for the most part, by her mother's face – albeit a wearier one. Perhaps she wonders why we don't go swimming. Or why she hasn't seen another little face like hers for a while. Or why her father, a doctor, is these days rarely back in time for her bath.

More likely, she doesn't wonder. She sleeps, and feeds, and plays with her jungle gym, blissfully unaware of how life has been upended across the globe. Our unassailable civilisation has been stripped bare, replaced by this fragile, ghostlike existence where we wave shyly at the delivery man from the window and interrupt each other over Zoom.

For her, however, the only difference is that her routine has just moved further indoors.

I spent the first few days batting away the anxiety swirling in the pit of my stomach. We turned inward as the outside world retreated, an unfathomable stillness settling around us. Life stopped in the blink of an eye. We were taken aback when the Premier League was cancelled, but two weeks later crossing the street to keep our distance was normal behaviour.

Yet still my baby smiles at me in the way she always has. And I have begun to watch her habits more closely than before.

As the rest of us fill our days with background noise, she prefers the silence. The birds tweeting outside, or the letterbox rattling makes her head turn instantly, as she ponders the new sound that has penetrated her bubble. There may be fewer faces to examine on our walks, but she absorbs herself in the beauty of the flowers, the trees and the faded facades of painted houses. Homemade rattles of rice-filled plastic bottles steal her curiosity, as she explores every corner and possible sound effect. She doesn't get FOMO. She lives with a contracted horizon of just a few hours.

For many of us, the hardest part of this pandemic is the lack of control. In a world where we were used to things appearing at the touch of a button, escaping to new scenery with a few clicks and filling our hours with a hum of productivity, the control seized from us feels like a raid on something precious that we had never realised was precious before.

As I watch my baby each day, I know we can control one thing at least: our response to this. She does it well: savouring the stillness, fascinated by details and finding pleasure in the little things. I watch her tolerate the empty days, not worrying about tomorrow or wallowing in yesterday, but staying present in each and every moment . . . and I realise I have much to learn from her.

When this ends, the dresses in her drawer will no longer fit. But I will smile, knowing that while our society, our economy, our productivity, our minds, our achievements and our dreams were forced to slow down, the growth of a little baby continued, unhindered.

Rhian
The Thermometer

30 March 2020

When Proust ate a madeleine, it transported him back to his blissful childhood. My prompt's more prosaic than a fancy cake: the thermometer I'm using to check that I haven't got a Covid-19-induced temperature. And rather than a joyful time, it takes me to a harrowing and peculiar year: 2013, when I got breast cancer.

In the six months after my diagnosis I had the full monty: surgery, chemo, radiotherapy. I also lost my hair, ate my own weight in gummy bears, got married. I had to take my temperature twice a day as chemo made me neutropenic (my white blood cells died) and vulnerable to infection. Twice I was rushed to hospital to be pumped full of antibiotics. One of those times was on my daughter's fourteenth birthday and I can see her now, sobbing on a nurse's shoulder in Oncology.

Neutropenia also delayed the next round of chemo, so I was doubly anxious to avoid it. At least twice a day I'd stick the digital thermometer under my tongue and wait for the beep, then hold my breath. A normal reading put me one step closer to the whole ghastly business being over. A high reading had me repeating it every ten minutes, getting progressively more anxious.

I hadn't thought about the thermometer in years. I wasn't even sure we'd still got it, as we'd moved house years ago. But somehow it had survived, for when Covid-19 started to look like something to worry about I managed to find it in a drawer. Using it sent me straight back to 2013; the intervening years fell away. I could feel our old house's bumpy kitchen lino under my feet and see the red chair (long since dumped) that I used to sit in when I had chemo.

I railed, then, against the way the thermometer whooshed me back to my cancer year. I've worked hard to get over it – my gym T-shirt reads, 'I'm a cancer survivor, what's your superpower?' – and I no longer feel defined by it. But Covid-19 has changed all that. Not only does the thermometer act like a cancer-sensitive lightning rod for my memories, I'm now classed as a vulnerable person. I think about this as I stand in the queue for the first hour of Waitrose's opening, a careful two metres away from everyone else, and decide wryly that my vulnerable status has some benefits: at least I'll get first dibs on that morning's delivery of loo rolls.

Richard
A Grandmother's Wisdom

21 March 2020

I was brought up to believe that during times of national crisis there were two occupations that would always survive: the brewers and the entertainers. This wisdom was passed to me by my grandmother who was too much of a lady to mention the oldest profession. She had survived two world wars and a depression, been widowed twice, and had more bad luck than any one person really deserves. In her later days she spent much of her time in the kitchen telling my sister and me stories from her long life, and would often comment, 'The music halls never closed, and there was always beer.' She knew what she was talking about. She was our reference point, our source of wisdom and truth.

At the time, I was still at the 'What do you want to be when you grow up' stage of life and it was not until many years later, having spectacularly failed at school and finding myself in need of a job, that I was reminded of her hypothesis. Obviously, the professions could not be a choice for me. Dr Beeching had demolished the railways, so engine driver was out, and anyway diesel had replaced steam and the allure had gone with it. Then again, this was the late 1960s and I was a baby-boomer, the luckiest and possibly most deluded generation that ever existed. This was the post-war age, a time brimming with optimism where the old ways of class and privilege had given in to the new reality, and a classless future beckoned. We were convinced that we really could change the world. There would be truth, equality and fairness; peace and love would prevail; all would be well. And our obsession, and the vehicle for this truth, was music. As the 1960s gave way to the 1970s, live music was seemingly everywhere. And where there was music, there was usually beer. So there were Granny's two career opportunities, with Granny's added job security, all nicely wrapped up in one package, staring me in the face.

I didn't really fancy the actual work involved in brewing, much as I liked the product, as it seemed to involve getting up early and having a degree of discipline for which I was ill suited. Whereas all the musicians I knew got up late and stayed up late having fun. And so I ran away to join the rock 'n' roll circus. Not having a musical bone in my body, I was firmly in the crew camp, a backstage boy, and I haven't been seriously out of work since.

However, like actors, most people in the music industry spend a lot of time resting. The bills, though, still have to be paid and road crew are nothing if not versatile. Consequently, my CV reads like the old 'situations vacant' page of the *Evening Standard* during a jobs boom. There's not what you would call a formal career path in the music business. Promotion can be as much to do with who you meet and luck, as ability. But I'd like to think that consistent progress through the ranks is an indication of competence at the very least. I have worked my way through various depressions, recessions and changes of musical tastes and the birth of super stardom. And partly by luck, partly from judgement, I have managed to survive the excesses that did for many of my contemporaries. The business develops and the world changes.

Today's road crews and event technicians are professionals and much more sensible. The business has grown up. It is a relatively small family and we meet during bursts of intense and hectic activity before moving on to the next show and disappearing just as quickly. Many of us meet at the major events and have an opportunity to compare notes on what has happened since last time.

Fifty years on I'm poacher turned gamekeeper – renegade rock 'n' roll wide boy turned health-and-safety consultant. Glastonbury Festival is usually my first event of the season and two days ago, along with countless other events, it was cancelled. Over the last week just about everyone in my touring and festival family is out of work. Performers and the technical crews alike. And we have no idea when people will once again be allowed to fill the arenas, dance in the fields and revel en masse, in the company of like-minded souls.

We have survived straitened times before. We must accept that we are where we are and that this too shall pass. I try to be sanguine, but I am having a hard time coming to terms with the fact that Granny was wrong.

Emily Rose

Lone Twin

23 March 2020

Finally, I feel normal. The self-imposed solitude I've practised for years now has a name. I'm no longer unsociable, a bid odd – I'm self-isolating.

They say that anyone who's lost a twin, particularly an identical twin, never recovers. Having lost my twin sister at a very young age, I think this may be true. The lone twin tends to be a loner. Even at primary school, I preferred to play on my own. As a lone twin, I appreciate one-to-one relationships and am at a loss in groups. I hate crowds and noisy parties. And when it comes to intimate relationships, the constant longing for a replacement for the lost twin can cause tension: the demands for closeness are just too great. As in my case, this may result in a breakdown of the relationship.

So for some years now, I've found myself living alone – the odd woman who always goes about solo, accompanied only by her dog – pleasant enough, but not really fitting in. Behind my back, people probably say the dog must be a replacement for the child I never had. But she's not. If the dog is a replacement for anyone, it's for the twin sister I did have.

Now my solitary behaviour has become the social norm, condoned, even prescribed by the government. Responsible conduct. Now if I don't want to attend the party or sit with my friends in a crowded pub, I'm practising 'social distancing', I'm being considerate, a good citizen. The result is that I feel more at ease with myself than I have for years. This doesn't mean I don't sympathise with others for whom this isolation is new and alien. I've resolved to call one of my friends or neighbours every day to ask how they're doing, to let them know that I care. This is working well. A phone call is by definition one-to-one and people seem to appreciate the thought.

To all lone twins and other natural self-isolators I would say, This is our time. Enjoy it, but remember also to pick up the phone and support someone 'normal' who is no longer in their comfort zone.

Susan

The Online Delivery

01 May 2020

I'd been watching the clock all morning and now it ticked into the necessary next hour. A strange nervousness fluttered through me. This was the culmination of days of planning and waiting: the arrival of the online shopping delivery.

Securing a slot had provided an incredible sense of achievement. It came from hours spent logging on to the supermarket app, repeatedly scrolling across the screen only to be greeted each time by the same disappointing message of 'unavailable'. One final attempt hadn't prepared me for the utter surprise as a date with times was shown as available. A sudden rush of adrenaline and almost panic overtook me. Clicking on to a slot, it was confirmed by a bag of apples in the basket.

Winning the golden ticket was a matter of urgency, as my diabetic husband had been told he needed to be shielded, making going to the shops impossible.

Days ensued of planning menus, identifying what was needed and calculating how long this shop would need to last, until list to hand, we logged in to order the chosen items – only to meet other disappointments. Tinned tomatoes? Unavailable. Flour? Unavailable. Toilet rolls? Unavailable, and only three bananas permitted. It was all part of the strange and rationed world of Covid-19.

So the hour arrived. With only fifteen minutes remaining of the allotted slot, my husband, who'd been patrolling the front window, announced, 'It's here!' as the blue and white van pulled up outside our house. Craig, a smiling knight in shining armour, greeted us and cheerily asked how we were, a thoughtful gesture in this time-slot sensitive world. Making a human chain we worked like a well-drilled team, emptying the delivery trays one by one. Then it was done. Craig waved and drove off.

Like children on Christmas morning we un-packed the bags, almost squealing with delight at the products we'd hoped for being there yet just as grateful with the substitutions made by our unknown packer. Crunchy Nut Cornflakes instead of Weetabix was certainly an alternative we liked!

We've reflected on this strange lockdown time, and on how we crave mundane chores like shopping and a return to 'normal'. But not a return to a 'normal' that includes unsung heroes like Craig or the anonymous packers being on poor contracts and low pay.

For now, I reach for my phone, log on to the App and enter the lottery again.

Michael
A School's Response
02 May 2020

Each day I drive a different route to school. I'm determined to avoid anything that might be considered a routine.

During lockdown I want to bring as much variety as possible into my life. I never set the alarm for the same time and I adjust my bathroom routines and vary the hygiene merchandise I use. The cabinet shelves are now fuller than during any previous stage of my life. Thank goodness for online ordering.

I no longer worry about moving noiselessly around the house at five thirty in the morning as my partner and daughter have decamped to be with Grandma. No more cuddles. I live alone and haven't caressed or embraced anyone for a month and a half.

Those closest to me are worried that my head-teacher duties – opening school every day and being around the children of key workers and our most vulnerable youngsters – will put them at risk. They may well be right.

I email my staff two times every day – to recount the comings and goings of daily school life but also to share how hard each colleague is working for the benefit of our children and their families. I digress and ramble and natter with intent. We're working in separate teams in a split rota of dedication, and I want to ensure feelings of joint purpose and collectiveness continue.

We open at seven in the morning and close at six in the evening and numbers of children coming into school differ each day. Sometimes as many as thirty, sometimes only half that number. Their days are filled with arts and crafts and models and stories and poetry and dance and cricket and baking and hot chocolate and big school lunches.

Our community may be socially distancing but it continues to be emotionally close. We may have to separate out in classrooms and avoid each other in corridors but we compensate with smiles and shouts and lots of signing. The children find it remarkably easy to apply the two-metre rule.

We have also found many ways to keep in touch with the wider community. Hundreds of Facebook updates every day, both sent out and received. There's food and work-pack deliveries, and voucher transfers. There are calls to children and families by phone and over FaceTime, there are online certificate assemblies to compere and an old-fashioned handwritten letter for all. There is no routine. There is change and challenge and our very best possible school response.

Jo

So Many Different Lengths of Time

18 March 2020

My lovely brother died two weeks ago. We bury him tomorrow. His death wasn't unexpected – he received his diagnosis of cancer in June last year, and we knew that it was aggressive and advanced. None of us was ready for him to go. He was a brilliant and enthusiastic lover of life. He squeezed every last drop out of his final months and he helped us all to adjust to his diagnosis and its inevitable outcome with his matter-of-fact approach.

His sons and wife (a hastily arranged but beautiful wedding in the summer with every friend and relative contributing to the colourful celebration) helped him to plan his funeral in what must have been a searingly painful process. He went to the wildflower meadow and chose his plot, overlooking the hills he loved so much. He chose the music and the readings. He made the whole thing as easy for us all as possible. Two weeks ago things were so different. Two weeks ago, we said our final goodbyes to him, stroking his head and holding his hand, before walking away from his hospice bed. We held his children close and we cried onto each other's shoulders. It felt as though we had been cast adrift, and were clinging on to each other to stay afloat.

When we say goodbye tomorrow, can I hold my mum, his mum, as she cries? Can I hug his dad, my dad? Can we even squeeze hands to show how much we care, how much pain we are in?

We are preparing as best we can. My 5-litre bottle of hand sanitiser is arriving today to make sure everyone can clean their hands. As I work on the front line in healthcare, I won't be hugging anyone except my husband and kids who are exposed to me every day. Some of my friends in the NHS are no longer even kissing their kids goodnight, but I can't take that comfort away from mine as they say goodbye to their beloved uncle. How can I tell my mum and dad that I am worried about them going to their own son's funeral? In my attempt to keep people safe I know I will appear standoffish and maybe people will think I am over-reacting, drawing attention to myself, even being cold.

In truth, I am utterly, utterly, heartbroken. My instinct is to be close to those in emotional distress. I am a hugger. The prospect of not being able to physically support my loved ones is making this difficult time even more distressing. But what can we do? We must look after each other. We must try to minimise the spread. We must socially distance.

At the funeral I will be reading Brian Patten's 'So Many Different Lengths of Time'. It has helped me so much in these dark days. I hope it will help others to see that while we cannot hold each other at the moment, we can hold my brother in our memories and we will come through.

Toby
I Want to Pedal

08 April 2020

I want to pedal but I don't want to be judged for it. I'm surprised by how strong the urge is to go for a bike ride, but equally by how agonising the decision has become on whether it's the right thing to do in 'these times'. Sure, I can rationalise it. The Deputy Chief Medical Officer, no less, said only last week that we should get out and use our exercise time. Michael Gove suggested that forty-five minutes of cycling was about right – 'depending on fitness level'. If my lungs are in good shape, and they need to be for these Derbyshire hills, that's got to help if I get ill, surely? Less strain on the NHS and all that.

Curbar Edge isn't a remote beauty spot for me, it's at the top of the hill. Ten minutes in the car, maybe twice that on my bike if I try hard. I rock climb there regularly. Or at least I did. We take the kids for walks there. And yet . . . it's also the scene of Derbyshire police's now-infamous drone-footage tweet. If I ride my bike up there can I expect a drone with blue lights to come and film me? To become hashtag fodder on social media?

That's not really what is causing the agonising; it is the pleas from stretched frontline-NHS staff asking us to stay home and give them a fighting chance to beat this horror. My cousin is a senior nurse running what used to be a paediatric ICU at one of the big London hospitals, now just 'an ICU' because they are taking adults as well. She posted a selfie this morning, dressed in her full PPE. She thinks she is just doing her job, but I want her to know how incredibly proud of her I am, and how grateful we all are for the thousands like her across the UK, all 'just doing their jobs'. I don't want to do anything that would make the jobs of people like her any harder than they already are.

I used to get my cycling fix commuting to the school where I teach. It kept me fit, and perhaps set a good example, and many of my students seemed to find it vaguely amusing. But the school year crashed to an end two weeks ago, in the strangest of days, one filled with unexpected emotions and tears, particularly for my Y13 students and Y11 form as we realised this was it. All their work, and all my teaching to ready them for their exams, had dispersed into the air like micro droplets from a dry cough.

I now sit at home trying to think of ways to teach kids I can't see and trying to make sure my own kids are OK. I worry about my 'high risk group' parents far away, about friends on the NHS frontlines, and about whether riding my bike for an hour of peace is the right thing to do. Daffodils bloom in the sunny shelter of drystone walls, lapwings dance up on the high moors, kestrels and buzzards patrol the wooded dales and fields in the valley below my house. Cyclists, walkers and runners you meet out are all unfailingly friendly, even as we pass each other on opposite sides of the road or trail. Physical distance, yes, but a newly found social closeness.

All just an hour from my front door. With full use of well-tuned brakes on the descents to keep it all very 'sensible'. I think that's OK. Isn't it?

Sara

Passover in Lockdown

07 April 2020

Lockdown has happened at an interesting time for Jewish people. Tonight, Passover begins – the festival of our freedom from slavery in ancient Egypt. The laws of the festival dictate that for eight days we must not own or consume chametz, leaven. Not even a crumb of bread is allowed in the food we eat. To prepare for this, we clean our homes with great care. Fridges and freezers are emptied; tables and chairs are scrubbed; even children's toys are given a once over, and certain items deemed impossible to clean are put away in a cupboard that will remain closed for the whole festival.

When lockdown happened my mind jumped immediately to one thought – how on earth am I going to clean for Passover this year? Usually – at least in our house – the bulk of cleaning happens while the children are at school. I put the radio on, arm myself with Marigolds and sponges, and get to work. There is a certain pleasant, meditative quality to it; I am not embarrassed to admit that I quite enjoy it. But this year? How do you clean a fridge and an oven when you are feeding five people three meals a day, plus snacks in between? Well, it turns out that you can, but you can forget about the meditation.

Every year there are quips about how the real freedom we are celebrating is not actually the Exodus, but in fact the freedom from finally having finished all that cleaning. But this year, when we sit around our Passover table, just the five members of our household, and none of the extra guests we usually invite, we will, I suspect, take more than a moment to ponder the meaning of freedom at a time when we are prisoners in our own homes. The Passover meal is preceded by the recitation of the *Haggadah*, the book telling the story of the Exodus. It begins with a statement urging all who are hungry to come and eat. Inviting family and strangers to the Passover table is intrinsic to this festival – more so than for any other festival in the course of the Jewish year. But this year the stranger must remain in their isolation, we in ours. Sadly, the generations of families that usually spend this festival together, this year, will not.

There is a lot of soul searching going on in the religious Jewish community, about what this crisis means and why it could be happening. There are, of course, no concrete answers. But one thing is certain – those of us who, please G-d, live through this crisis will never think of the words 'Festival of our Freedom' in the same way again.

Kate

To the Greenhouse

10 April 2020

My friends and family keep asking me if I'll join in a Zoom, Houseparty, FaceTime chat, virtual coffee time or drinks party. I don't really want to. I'm actually enjoying the social isolation, aside from the bluster and bickering my teenagers bring to my life. My life has been a rollercoaster, emotionally, financially, and in every other imaginable way, since my husband suddenly died two and a half years ago, and I am now able to take the time I should have had then to sit back and reflect. After his death I had to wind up his business, get my children off to school, and get my own business going in order to keep a roof over our heads. It was all-consuming. Now I can take a breath.

In the morning, I wake before the teenagers and I potter out to my greenhouse. My little dog, Dorothy, comes with me, my faithful companion, always at my side. I water my trays of seedlings, perhaps sow another tray or two and work out which ones I'll soon need to prick out. The smell of the compost and the stillness of the air, new life springing up all around me, brings everything into perspective. My husband built this green-house for me the year before he died. Little did he know it would maintain my sanity and bring so much gentle happiness to my soul. I'm a garden designer and, unable to go out to work at the moment, finally, I get to plant my own garden. I have no money coming in, but I'll have to worry about that later.

The teenagers eventually appear at various points throughout the day, and I feel guilty once again that the chat we'd had about structured days yesterday, and the day before, and the day before, keeps falling by the wayside, my seedlings having already had more of my attention than them. They don't seem to mind. As long as long as they're provided with meals and WiFi and I'm somewhere in the vicinity, all is well.

I consult the list I've made for my day and the week ahead. I always make a list on a Monday, and despite life being thrown up into the air, I've continued to do this. But now it's things like, 'paint back door, clear gutters to water butts, change everyone's sheets'. Anything to give myself a sense of achievement when I cross it off the list and make me feel as if I've earned my 'free' time, whatever that means.

I do some of the jobs on my list, admittedly avoiding the ones I really hate, and before long the WhatsApp will come. 'Thought we'd have drinks over a Zoom meeting later . . . here's the code.'

It's not that I don't love my family and friends. I really do. And I love talking to them on the phone. But it reminds me what a strange time this is, the disjointed and unnatural gatherings around laptops, trying to think about what to chat about when no one has really done anything since last time, and also reminding me that, unlike almost everyone I know, I am not hunkered down with my partner. While I am accustomed to this state of play, seeing friends and their part-ners on a screen makes them seem rose-tinted and an uncharacteristic, and unwelcome, jeal-ousy creeps in. My nineteen-year-old daughter, full of wisdom, reminds me that this is a stressful time for almost all couples and families, with difficult times being tackled for many less fortunate than us all behind closed doors. She is, of course, so right.

I have told my dear friends how I feel. They understand and so instead we have one-to-one chats on the phone, just every now and then. Despite its tragic origins, the time I have now, away from work, loved ones, wider family and friends, feels like a gift I must make the best possible use of, before the chaos of life resumes, as it surely eventually will. Until then, I'll look forward, with great hope and excitement, to catching up with my family and friends in person. No screen required.

Caroline

Going Up, Going Down

04 April 2020

Email from north London to a friend in Florida the day the lockdown began there.

Hi, lovely to chat last night and sorry if I made it all sound a bit grim, in fact for me personally things are fine!

The last two or three weeks, apart from being ill for a few days, have been a lovely opportunity to slow down, lie around watching box sets of *Mad Men*, tackle the garden and go for walks. We have had mostly glorious weather and I am relishing not having to race around with bags and papers from one place to the next.

And we're fine of course because we have space at home and don't have small children to entertain or educate.

We chat and have online drinks with friends, watch films. People share poetry, music and recipes, tell you where to buy yeast or flour or whatever and the best places to shop locally and online. I can do Pilates, with my teacher who's moved online, and a daily ballet warm-up to get me going. We go out once a day for a walk or bike ride.

On Thursday evenings people stand outside their front doors to applaud NHS workers, the vicar rings the church bell, people bang pots and let off fireworks – we live near a lot of hospitals – and many other nice things are happening.

This week has been harder, mainly because I am back at work, at home. We already know that many people are not as fortunate and that this lockdown will lead to terrible problems for some. I am finding out first-hand how some of my students are – it's so sad, one person with a garden has kept her children inside for three weeks because we have been told to stay indoors. Part of my work now really is just to contact those people, reassure them and make sure they have proper information. And of course, although the virus itself can affect anyone, the people who started out with less of everything will likely come out of this worse in the end, as always.

Anyway, here are some of my predictions and observations (mostly positive) so far!

GOING UP!

- Healthier house plants
- Lovelier gardens
- Delivery jobs
- Divorce rates (not yet but soon)
- Birth rates (ditto, in about nine months)

GOING DOWN!

- Newspaper travel supplements
- Coffee shops

THINGS WE USE MORE:

- Exercise clothes
- Bicycles
- Video conferencing apps

THINGS WE USE LESS:

- Handbags
- Make-up (possible exception, lipstick for video calls!)
- Work clothes
- Public transport

MAIN TOPICS OF CONVERSATION:

- Food
- Exercise
- Baking
- Gardening
- Poetry
- Art
- Music

WHAT WE HAVE MORE OF:

- Conversations with neighbours
- Cleaner air
- The sound of birdsong
- Time to stand and stare

Keep me posted
Love
xx

Phil

A Letter on Your First Birthday

13 April 2020

Your first birthday happens to have fallen on
Easter Sunday – a holiday weekend – when ordi-
narily the family would have gathered around
you and your parents to celebrate. Balloons, cakes,
hugs and kisses would have been the order of
the day, and you would perhaps have – in your
own small way – discerned the joy of the occasion, and the love of which you were the focus,
and the love with which you were embraced.

But this is no ordinary first birthday. This is
April 2020; and the country – the world – into
which you were born seems a distant memory.
Everything has changed, and a new normality
has both constrained and defined everyday life.
Friends and family no longer meet, embrace, and
progress together along life's path in a shared
kinship. All this we formerly took so easily for

granted. The time will come when we can do so once more, but that time is not now, not yet.

In future years, the older generation may talk of these times, recalling the apprehension, the insecurity, and the fear that now stalks the land – a folk memory preserved in the annals of the collective unconscious.

You, I hope, will experience nothing of this. The Easter weather shone brightly, and you have played in your paddling pool, splashing water without a care in the world. You have stared curiously at sand running through your tiny fingers in your sandpit. And you have gurgled with open delight on a first bike ride with your parents. As you smile and wave at video images of us – your grandparents – through the medium of modern technology, I can't help but wonder about your nascent understanding of the world about you. What kind of world do you – will you – inhabit? Will it be a world characterised by a new sense of shared community, of mutual destiny, with an understanding that each of us is only as strong as the weakest of us? I so hope that you will grow to maturity in a safer, kinder and less divided world.

Meanwhile, we will hold up a birthday banner for you to see, wave balloons, sing your birthday song, and participate electronically in this celebratory day of your young life. We will pretend that things are normal, even though they are not, in the hope that one day – another day – we can come together as people have always done, and as friends and families should. Supporting, reassuring and nurturing each other through the good times and the bad. Smiles, hugs and kisses will – once again – be the order of the day.

But, for now, with much love . . . happy birthday, Cleo!

Will You Isolate With Me?

01 April 2020

Will you isolate with me? I asked. *Sure*, he said.

Well, he actually said *claro*, because we live in Spain. I moved here two years ago from the UK because I was being stalked. I was terrified, it had been going on for a long time, there was a trial (he was found guilty), I was traumatised and wanted a new life. So I moved to the sea.

But it wasn't all sunshine and rainbows. Being stalked does terrible things to the mind. I was determined, though, not to let what happened define the rest of my life. I started to be grateful for everything I had and day by day, slowly slowly, things improved. Last summer I walked the whole of the Camino de Santiago, a wonderful, healing experience.

A year and a half after I moved here, I met him. A friend of a friend. We kissed, fell in love. An impossible love. A love I never thought I would ever have. Because I never thought I would be able to trust again.

And now here he is. Isolating with me in my flat with its beautiful terrace where we watch the blue skies as we sip on our morning coffee and nibble avocado on toast. I love him more and more every day. I feel enveloped by our romance. Like I'm floating.

And then we switch on the TV to be hit with an unspeakably terrible reality. Thousands more infections – which are probably just a fraction of the actual number – and hundreds of deaths. Every. Single. Day. I realise that each of those deaths is somebody's loved one. Somebody who is loved just as much as I love him.

I feel guilt. Immense guilt. How can I be so happy in our little cocoon when outside there is so much loss and pain?

Emma

I Felt I Should be Crying

03 April 2020

As we drove up to the gates, we could see they were locked. Pinned to the bars were several notices, giving instructions to visitors. At the top of one notice, in large red letters, was the word 'CORONAVIRUS'.

We waited a few moments, unsure what to do. A man appeared. He was wearing blue surgical gloves. I told him our appointment time, and who we were there for, and he opened the gates. As we drove slowly through, he explained that we couldn't enter the building yet, but we could wait outside. Following his gestured directions, we made our way up the long driveway, to the top of the hill.

We parked. Only two or three other cars were there. As I got out, I saw a robed figure in the main doorway, under the portico, waiting to greet us. He smiled gently, and we approached him, stopping at a safe distance away. We made small talk: what a chilly day it was; how his first wife had red hair, like me; that he loved Aker Bilk's 'Stranger on the Shore' and had it ready to play. The wind circled and I started to shiver.

'They'll be here any minute,' he said.

And they were. I turned around and saw that she'd arrived in the polished limousine. 'She's here,' I said, pointlessly. A man in a black hat and frockcoat got out of the car and smiled palely at me. Four more frockcoats slid her out of the vehicle. With smooth precision, they lifted her onto their shoulders. 'Follow behind,' said the black hat man.

As I turned to follow, through the heavy wooden doors and down the aisle, I looked behind at my three companions. Everyone looked sad, lost – well, this is what their eyes expressed. I couldn't see their mouths: like me, they were wearing facemasks.

The four of us took our places – spaced apart – on a wooden bench at the front of the room. All the other seats were empty. No-one else was permitted to attend.

We listened. Vaughan Williams' 'The Lark Ascending'. Prayers. Some readings from the King James Bible. The eulogy.

I felt I should be crying, like I'd cried three weeks ago, but I couldn't. It was all so . . . odd. The rich, soft melody of 'Stranger on the Shore' drifted across the almost-empty pews. Inside my mask I smiled at the vicar's kind words and final blessing.

'I really wanna see you, Lord, but it takes so long, my Lord.' As the final song played, we were ushered to the exit. I looked back at the coffin, the seats, the emptiness. I said a goodbye in my head, but I don't remember what it was.

Bewildered, I stepped outside into the cold. The vicar pumped hand sanitiser onto his palms and rubbed it thoroughly into his hands. 'It's the best we could do, in the circumstances,' he said. I said thank you, wanting to shake hands but knowing I couldn't. 'Thank you,' I repeated. There was nothing else to say.

As my eyes finally began to blur with tears, we left, driving back down the hill, out of the gates and home.

I'm sorry. It's not my fault, but I'm sorry anyway. There should have been more people there, but they were not allowed to come because they're old and vulnerable and they could catch this virus that's closed the world down. You missed it. You're safe from it now. Perhaps that's a blessing. If you had caught it, you would have suffered even more. I wanted it to feel like a funeral, to celebrate your life properly, but it didn't, and I couldn't, and I can't change anything. But even though there was almost no-one there, the vicar read out my words about you, and I chose your favourite songs, and before you died, at least I got to talk to you and tell you that I love you. I got to stroke your head, and kiss your frail skin, and thank you for everything you did for me.

Now, more than ever, that feels very, very precious.

Now, more than ever, I love you, Mum.

x

Xenia

A Birthday in Lockdown

03 April 2020

7 a.m.: Today is my ninety-third birthday and thanks to Covid-19 I'm confined to my house and unable to celebrate with family and friends. However, to be alive and still more or less mobile and compost mentis, is an achievement, or maybe just good luck, but anyway, I intend to celebrate it. I woke feeling very pleased, having had an exceptionally good night's sleep and interesting dreams of being at a dinner party, with wonderful conversation, that lasted so long that I finally returned home at 3 a.m. and had a lot of trouble finding the right keys to the door. What a strange dream and unusual to remember so much of it.

10 a.m.: I've had breakfast, a leisurely bath and am ready for the day. Having decided to celebrate despite the circumstances, I've abandoned the tracksuit I've been living in for the last couple of weeks and am wearing proper trousers

and the new jacket I bought recently. Since my mother's death I've always bought myself a present from her on my birthday, as I know she would have wished. The strange thing is that this year I can't think of a single thing I want to buy. Under normal circumstances, if I couldn't think of an object, I'd have a treat, like taking someone out to lunch or going to an exhibition, but thanks to Covid-19 that's impossible.

11 a.m.: I've had phone calls from three friends and opened my three birthday cards. I make a thermos of coffee and sit in the front garden so my daughter can come for a socially distant coffee. Thankfully she lives very close by, so we can meet outside fairly regularly. During our coffee the robins came out, waiting for the food I give them every morning, and a blackbird turned up. Then the postman arrived and delivered a long thin cardboard box which turned out to be flowers from my friend David. I was astonished for although he always remembers my birthday it's unusual for him to make a gesture like this.

12 p.m.: Three parcels arrive, birthday presents from my daughter. I'm too hungry to open them now, and as I have lunch ready in the oven

I'll save the pleasure of opening them till later. I'm having an amazing birthday!!!! Very happy.

1.30 p.m.: Wow, in the middle of lunch, the bell rings and there's another amazing bouquet of flowers from a dear old friend. My only sadness today has been a posting to say that he didn't get on to the last drug trial for his cancer and, in fact, it looks as though for the time being trials are stopping. I feel devastated for him. He has tried so hard to keep himself physically and mentally strong. Only an extraordinary person in these circumstances, and on morphine to keep the pain at bay, would think of sending birthday flowers to an old lady.

4 p.m.: I've found another vase and had more phone calls from friends and family plus a cup of ginger tea with the small cake from the posh bakery and frankly, I'm exhausted, so I'm going to lie down to rest for half an hour. Who would have thought spending one's birthday alone could be so tiring?

6 p.m.: My daughter has introduced me to Zoom and I've a call scheduled. I'm feeling a little apprehensive because it sounds complicated. Learning how to use FaceTime and Zoom in the same week is a bit much. I've also just had a

message from my granddaughter in Canada, who posted a very touching account of her relationship with me, which I absolutely don't deserve.

7 p.m.: Zoom took up a lot of time and, after various futile attempts, my son-in-law had to come over, wearing a mask and rubber gloves, and do a lot of things on my iPad, which I'd left for him in the porch. Suddenly I was able to talk to all the grandchildren, together on one screen. Quite an amazing experience. When I was a child all we had was a radio and even that was fairly novel for most people. I first experienced the marvel of television at the age of twelve. It was a large boxy piece of furniture with a very small screen and for about two hours a day there was broadcasting in black and white. My mother and I had just arrived from Vienna, escaping from Hitler, and we were temporarily living, with my mother's aunt, in the flats above the John Barnes department store. That was in 1938 and then the war happened, so no television happened again until after that. In my wildest dreams I couldn't have imagined then what I experienced on Zoom today.

7.30 p.m.: I've opened a half bottle of Prosecco and a packet of smoked salmon, cut a lemon in half and am signing off for the time being because alcohol is likely to make me incoherent.

8.30 p.m.: I enjoyed my supper, then watched half a programme on zoo animals and ate a large chunk of my birthday chocolate egg. I've decided to put the whole day's dirty dishes into the dishwasher instead of doing the washing up, as I usually would, and then watch the only programme on TV that's of interest at 9 o' clock.

10.30 p.m.: A last thought before going to bed. Living through this coronavirus epidemic, right at the end of my life, is a very unexpected experience, and having lived through momentous happenings at the start of my life, the Holocaust and World War Two, it seems right to go through another momentous experience at the end. Perhaps we should all re-read *Love in the Time of Cholera* by Gabriel García Márquez.

Jane

The Feeling of Being Close

06 April 2020

My youngest son is due to finish primary school in July. This milestone marks a significant shift in family life. From September, all three boys will be up and out by seven thirty, on the train across London to school, returning tired and hungry at half four.

Some parents I know are rejoicing in what they expect to be an increase in freedom, as their offspring continue to grow and gain independence. 'All your kids at secondary school, it'll be great,' they say. 'Before you know it, they'll be leaving home – you'll get your life back!'

This isn't how I feel. It's a cliché, I know, but I just can't believe how quickly the time has gone. I trawl through old family photos and videos, marvelling at their toddler perfection. At the time I was stressed and exhausted, having had three kids in four years. It wasn't fun when it was happening, but now it's gone, the memories make me ache.

Pre-lockdown, I'd feel teary looking at calendar dates for 'Year 6 Leavers' Assembly' and 'Secondary School Induction Morning'. I'd been making extra efforts to leave work early to collect him from the gates at least twice a week, so I could enjoy his company on the walk home, before he morphed into a grunting, silent teenager like his brothers, whose main words to me are 'OK Boomer' whenever I voice an opinion, or ask them to do something.

But now? Now they're here all day. They're around. I'm responsible for feeding them, all meals. They seek me out, they talk to me, ask me what I'm doing on the computer, how work is going, what we're doing later on, shall they wash the dog, who's turn is it to run the hoover round? They fight and laugh and shout and wrestle. They rack up an obscene body count on some game they swear blind is age appropriate.

No more 6.30 a.m. starts and commutes to school across town. The older two get up between ten and eleven, the youngest, around half nine. Two teens and a tween. All of us on a go-slow. I feel like I'm borrowing this time from them, when they should be ignoring me and I should be hurtling towards obsolescence, like all good parents.

Instead, though, it reminds me of when they were little, and used to follow me around. All of us together, all day. Back then I couldn't wait for it to end. Now, I've been given a second chance for a short period, to snatch again the feeling of my children being close.

My Hope is Intact (Just)

07 April 2020

I have been scratched, pinched, hit or yelled at every day.

I am almost forty, a mother for over a decade, and the perpetrator is my youngest daughter.

How can I be held to ransom by someone so small?

Feelings of impotence are not uncommon during this pandemic. How do I help – when I can't leave my house? What can I do – when I am not a key worker?

My child's chaotic episodes only serve to remind me how very limited I am, how futile my resources.

I have a Cambridge University education, but I fail to find the words to finish a sentence by the end of the day. I am a qualified accountant, but I cannot balance the needs with the demands.

Because I share a house with my husband, three children, and a big raging ball of trauma.

My youngest daughter came to us a toddler, having experienced care so poor it makes my heart crack in two. Through absolutely no fault of her own, she carries this trauma: an ugly monster, which flourishes amidst uncertainty, worry and change.

This trauma had been tamed; school had become a joy. After rocky years, she was starting to thrive.

But this virus has stolen the progress and joy and given trauma a space to spread its wings and stretch out its tentacles once again.

To a child who has already lost so much, who already knows that people don't always come back, how do I reassure her that she will see her friends and her grandparents again? To a child wired for danger, how do I urge her to wash her hands constantly without instilling fear? To a child who trusts no one, how can I expect her to do as I say?

'I feel like I am in the rain, standing in a puddle with my wellies full of water. All on my own.'

She told me this going to bed one evening in the first week of school closures. And just like that she managed to convey her felt terror.

So, if I'm hit, bitten or scratched, so be it. We're not going to let the trauma, or the virus, take away the truth: she is not alone. You are not alone. We are not alone.

Amidst the chaos we go for bike rides, play tennis in the garden, bake cakes. Each lovely thing is punctuated by the raging monster, but we will do them anyway. We won't let the monsters or the fear triumph. Even if the neighbours can hear.

Because as I look ahead to Easter Sunday, I remember that someone has already triumphed over brokenness, fear and even death. So, our hope is intact. My arms, my confidence, my heart may be bruised. But my hope is intact.

Terry

The Trials of Video-Calling

08 May 2020

I am looking up my father's nostrils. It's not a pretty sight.

I live 100 miles away and am trying to teach him how to video call.

My father is eighty-six. Prior to the lockdown he owned an ancient brick of a mobile phone. You could never reach him on it.

'I switch it on when I need to make a call.' Which is never, as he is old school and uses his landline. After 6 p.m., obviously, as 'daytime calls cost more.'

It's the week before lockdown.

'Come and stay with us, Dad.'

'Not at all, it'll be over in no time. I'm quite happy as I am. Thank you.'

My dad survived the Asian 'flu of 1957, and malaria in West Africa. Covid-19 is not going to intimidate him.

My sister offers him her old iPhone. Having previously eschewed the very idea, he's now prepared to give it a go. However; his PAYG top-ups will not keep it going for long, so he is persuaded, reluctantly, to take out a contract. Now he can make and receive calls at any time of day.

I try one last appeal, to head north with me.

'I have a lovely flat, with a lovely view of the park, and it doesn't smell of pig shit. Thank you.'

Perhaps I shouldn't have mentioned that the farmers are muck spreading across the Mearns right now, and the smell of fertilizer is eye watering.

I arrive home and call him. No answer. I try again. I call his landline.

'I AM ANSWERING!' He sounds frustrated. 'I AM PRESSING THE BUTTON BUT IT JUST KEEPS RINGING!'

'You have to swipe it, Dad.'

'What do you mean, "swipe it"?'

'You put your finger on the button and swish it upwards.'

It doesn't help that I own a Samsung Galaxy and don't know the layout of his iPhone.

We progress to WhatsApp. Further frustrations. This is not going well.

I call the landline daily and we do a tutorial, with me googling iPhone 6 on my computer. I really know no better than he does.

The days slip by. I'm about to give the old boy a call when my mobile begins to ring. It says 'Dad' on the screen. I answer, and see a thumb and his kitchen ceiling, and I burst out laughing. He's cracked it!

ISOLATION

Kim & Matt

Hope

08 May 2020

My husband and I lost our darling daughter, Hope, on 10 April 2020. She was only alive for twenty-eight short days but in that time she enriched our lives so much. Her devastating loss was magnified by the current coronavirus pandemic. Here is ours and Hope's story.

During our twenty-week scan we received the life-altering news that our baby girl had complicated heart problems. She was due to be seen by the doctors at Great Ormond Street and we built a relationship with nurses, surgeons and counsellors there, who all agreed a plan for Hope's treatment. Induction was scheduled at UCLH for 9 March with Hope to be transferred to GOSH shortly after birth for specialist care. However, a cardiologist at GOSH was diagnosed with Covid-19 and they were forced to close the hospital to new admissions. A new plan was arranged, and I was finally induced on 12 March with Hope's care being transferred to the team at the Evelina London Children's Hospital. Hope was born on 13 March after an emergency C-section because of her blood pressure dropping suddenly. Due to the new hospital restrictions, only my husband was permitted to be by my side, with my mother turned away upon our arrival at UCLH. Hope was transferred to the Evelina at St Thomas' along with my husband, separating me from my baby who I'd only been able to hold for approximately half an hour.

I was diagnosed with a pulmonary embolism on my left lung, which meant that I had to remain in hospital for almost a week after her birth. I requested to be transferred to St.Thomas' Hospital to be closer to my baby, and even though both hospitals attempted to do this it was not possible due to ever tightening virus controls. I had my husband on one side of London with our very poorly baby girl awaiting imminent surgery and myself in another with my own health complications wanting more than anything for us to be reunited as a three.

During her stay in hospital, we barely got any time as a family of three; restrictions on visitors on the ward meant that only one parent was allowed to be at her bedside, therefore we have only a few precious memories and photographs of our time together as a family. Alongside the visiting restrictions, the kind, caring staff had to adhere to strict PPE protocols meaning that they were unable to offer their usual level of warmth, empathy and close support. The atmosphere within the hospital became more fraught with lots of questioning and security checks through-out, which was then magnified further when the Prime Minister was admitted and armed police patrolled the building.

Only three days old, Hope had a successful first surgery. After two weeks of recovery from that, we received the good news that she would soon be well enough to go home. We couldn't believe that the day we had been longing for was finally here and we could start to put our time in hospital behind us. A couple of days later, how-ever, things began to take a turn for the worst when one of her discharge scans showed that she no longer had any blood flow to her left lung. They attempted to fix the vessel via a keyhole procedure, but it was too difficult. Further open heart surgery was necessary. That seemingly went well, and the surgeon was happy with how it had gone, but five hours post-surgery her blood pressure dropped and the doctors in PICU couldn't revive her. We lost our precious beautiful baby girl. The immense pain and hurt that came over us was like nothing we had ever felt. We were drowning and no matter how hard we tried, we couldn't come up for air. Our lives completely collapsed. Hope endured so much in her little life but was always so calm and brave! Our grief was compounded by the fact that the doctors were unable to offer us a cause of death and she had to go to the coroner for a post-mortem to attempt to understand why she passed. Our family never met her alive and were only allowed to see her after she had died. We were (and still are) unable to have our loved ones around us to support us during our time of need.

The pain of arranging her funeral was something neither I nor my husband thought we would ever have to go through. It took over three weeks for her body to be taken into the care of the funeral directors, as mortuaries were full to capacity. Due to coronavirus restrictions, her funeral will be a basic affair with only immediate family permitted to attend. A weblink will be available to friends and family who wish to 'attend' the service online.

Our journey through the last ten months was excruciatingly hard but we always had 'Hope'. We chose her name to signify our belief that no matter what was thrown at us or what we were told by professionals, we would always have hope that there would be light at the end.

Unfortunately for us, all 'Hope' is currently lost. Losing a child is the hardest thing that any human must endure, yet somehow it has been made even worse by the situation that the world finds itself in.

Alison

Sorting Through Photographs

29 April 2020

'This is going to get worse before it gets better' – words to strike fear into the heart. A medical procedure, decorating a room, a reorganisation at work? Actually, none of the above. Merely: Sorting Out the Photographs. Those that hide in drawers, skulk on shelves, lurk in carrier bags. One such bag had been in the deep, dark cupboard under the stairs for several years. My brother gave it to me, after clearing out the family home when our mother died. To be fair, he had gone through Mum's photos and thrown away many, without troubling me. These were a selection he thought might be of interest. There they were, photographs gathered from the four corners of my house, and now spread out on the sitting-room floor. How to categorise? Photos of the Significant Holidays were, in fact, already in albums, these being before the advent of iPhones.

They were resolutely not reviewed and went straight into a large box. I bought four plastic boxes into which to put an album each and memorabilia (school reports, certificates etc), for my three siblings and me. Starting on Monday, it took three days (in between walks, shopping, meals etc) to assign everything a home. A few photos were abstracted to frame, and a few thrown away – mainly the sepia prints taken at the coast of people unknown, for there is no one left to tell me who they were. Three labelled boxes sit in a spare wardrobe, ready to be removed or reviewed – or not – at some unspecified time in the future. The point of today's chronicle is to tell you that, contrary to Marie Kondo and similar, there is a value in keeping your photos in carrier bags. Go through them: you will laugh, cry – reminisce, even, if you are lucky enough to have someone with whom to do this. But then: put them back. You will have saved several days of hard, fiddly work, racking your brains wondering who people were, and maybe saved money on extra storage. You can still look at your photos any time you like. At some time, unspecified, in the future, someone, not you, will go through the photos. Maybe they will look at them, laugh, cry, reminisce. They may even abstract a few to frame. But probably, and lightly, they will toss most into a bin.

Julie

Compliance and Defiance

01 May 2020

What a difference a month makes, thirty-one long days, 744 hours, especially in lockdown.

April Fools' Day 2020, celebrating the first birthday of my second granddaughter. A milestone moment, but instead of joining together with family at the seaside, spending time exploring sand, sea and seals, it was a birthday in isolation. Presents delivered to the doorstep, video calls to sing 'Happy Birthday', photos of a cake-smeared face and little fingers tugging wonderingly on a pink helium balloon. She's too young to remember this subsequently, but the ache will remain in our hearts that we weren't there, that the photographs won't reflect the love we feel for her and were prevented from showing with hugs and kisses.

Fast forward to the first of May and a reunion occurs at the graveside of my father. From bittersweet celebratory birthday to bittersweet commemorative funeral, united again in lockdown only because of the unexpected death of the patriarch of the family over the Easter weekend.

His death had nothing to do with Covid-19, rather an accidental fall downstairs at his home fracturing his neck instantly, another statistic for ONS, but not one to earn the condolences of any government minister on any daily briefing. Our days since Easter have been filled with busyness: notifying people, sorting through paperwork, organising a twenty-minute graveside ceremony attended by immediate family only, emptying a house he lived in for fifty-six years, dealing with probate. When we look back on lockdown in years to come, these two dates will always be etched on our minds. Life and death, both remembered in vastly different ways to the usual; the poignancy of death at Easter, the hope of resurrection framing this reunion.

An ordinary family, marking milestones in extraordinary ways, compliance and defiance combined as we sing my father's favourite Christmas carol at the beginning of May. Surreal? As is everything in lockdown. 'We isolate so we can gather again'? Our next family gathering will now be in heaven. This hope sustains us through the long days of grief.

James

They Called Us, and We Went

13 May 2020

There was no air flow in the room, it was hot and too many of us were present. I was itching to leave until a surprise came at the medical consultants' coronavirus meeting in March. Dermatology (with Rheumatology, 'the ologies') was the first medical speciality to be joining Respiratory on what was currently our Trust's only 'Covid ward'. Perhaps a joke, a mistake, had I missed something while worrying about social distancing and air flow? It soon became clear however that this was 'the plan' – and why. The whole hospital was predicted in a few weeks' time to be full of coronavirus cases. More worrying if possible, so were the corridors and car parks. So why move around other medical teams from their base wards, when they too would be overwhelmed shortly. Moving dermatology into the 'first breech' made sense, the least disruption.

There were a few more days to absorb this 'change' in our practice, go over some online training and prepare Dermatology for the months ahead. Another doctor and I were soon on the ward. It was a daily physical, intellectual and emotional act of defiance against the coronavirus pandemic creeping our way. A scramble against the predicted peak. Adrenaline, sadness and also fear – unavoidable from the multiple media outlets: images and reports from as nearby as Italy. What might we bring home to our families? What if we couldn't go home?

So, some tears, which have never come easily before, in the car on the way to the donning and doffing. The radio reports providing no hope, relief or respite. Then into scrubs, face tight and nose sore under PPE. Going to work like walking onto a movie set rather than a ward, zipped at entrance and exit. Patients passing away is nothing new, part of our job, but alone and apart from husbands and wives of forty years or more, surrounded by masks, gloves and gowns. It is difficult to know how to react or reflect on this . . .

However, we did enjoy our experience and made the most of it, I believe. Meeting and working so closely with medical colleagues of all grades, thinking in different ways. The S1Q3T3 spotted on an ECG with subsequent CTPA confirming a large PE and still being able to name the causes of a cavitating pneumonia (TANKS pneumonic), recruiting the second patient on to the RESPECT trial. The coffee was as terrible as I remembered on the wards, but after four hours in an FFP3 mask, it was like nectar. Then out into the fresh air and bright blue quiet skies. Each evening reading through journals online, covering the latest information on coronavirus, the next day discussing and implementing in real life.

We bore the worst of the local epidemic being on call over the long Easter weekend. By the end of that week the peak had passed, and things were no worse than when we first started on the wards. A few days more for reassurance and we were stood down. What a relief, what a bullet our hospital and county, perhaps country, seemed to have dodged. At least, when compared with the predictions just a few weeks previously.

Some asked if we volunteered with a hint of 'why would you and well, you asked for it' in their voice. But we did not ask. We were called and we went. I'm not so sure I would have volunteered, I'd have been afraid they might laugh! I'll never know. It's not as though there wasn't plenty of honest work to do in Dermatology, and still is. But we were there, we represented and we were prepared to stay for the duration. So now we are back in our offices in Dermatology. It's been a rollercoaster and it's taken some time to adjust back to office life.

It was a time of trust: in our government, our guidelines, our PPE, our training, our colleagues, ourselves. Most importantly the patients' trust in us. I trust we won't have to go through this again. If we do, I trust I, or those like me, will go again.

Beth

'Let's Dance'

01 May 2020

'So, let's dance, shall we?' Tomorrow will be our fortieth dance. One every evening since lockdown was announced. Me, Mum, my sister, my niece, my daughter. Three households, one WhatsApp call, one song, lots of chat. We started with 'Sweet Caroline', my choice, uplifting, and special to me for all sorts of reasons. But quickly Fay, organised as ever, who now has a list of potential choices pinned to her fridge (will it last as long as lockdown, we wonder?), began to make the lyrics more meaningful. Tomorrow, tomorrow, I love ya, tomorrow. Together in electric dreams. My blue sky. Girls just wanna have fun. Yesterday was Mum's choice. Elvis, 'Sea of Heartbreak'. Heartbreak that she can't see her grandchildren, like so many others. But we try not to cry, because we're healthy, we're lucky. We have gardens. Finally, Mum and Dad secure a Sainsbury's delivery. None of us is furloughed.

The list goes on. And so we stand in front of my phone and Ellen's phone, speaker at the ready with the music, then count down, and dance. My favourite so far was the can-can – good choice, Mum. And 'Waterloo', because of course ABBA has to feature. And for Steps – '5, 6, 7, 8' – Ellen taught me to line dance. Took me all day Saturday to learn, but then, what else did I have to do that was more urgent? Sometimes we persuade the boys to join us. If they do, we contribute £5 each per boy to Captain Tom, a lady supporting domestic violence victims, or another buying laptops for those in hospital. So many inspiring stories and people. Fran and Dave giving up their time to improve our booties or 'summer abs'. PPE for the NHS. The chap in our local pub running quizzes every day (no, we didn't win). Local charities otherwise overlooked.

So Dad, seventy-five and barely able to walk at the best of times, did the twist with Chubby Checker. Uncle Rich, who hates Christmas games, takes over the screen with his best moves, all in a good cause. It reminds me of my fiftieth, Ellen's eighteenth, all those occasions we really held each other and danced, and couldn't ever imagine we would celebrate Mum's seventy-sixth via Zoom. The dance that night: 'Happy Birthday'. What else?

Polly

Working from Home – with Children

27 April 2020

I have a pipe cleaner in my ear. There is glitter on the keys of my laptop. My arm is weighed down with a small bag of glitter-smeared stones.

The five-year-old is under the table in another room, hitting the floor and yelling because her dress 'isn't witchy enough'. I realise she hasn't eaten since 6 a.m., so she's *hangry*. The pipe cleaner jabs at my eardrum and I try to extract the three-year-old from my face, but I can't tell her off, because I'm trying to talk intelligently to a French client about how they should update their product range with more sustainable options.

I'm getting better at conference calls. The trick, I've discovered, is to say something really smart, a 'thought starter' as they say, and then immediately go on mute while everyone else on the call discusses your pearl of wisdom, allowing you a few seconds to look your child in the eye and suggest the next activity.

The five-year-old is still hitting the floor. There's a *clonk,* which sounds very much like the iPad being thrown across the room. I reposition the three-year-old so she can't reach my ear any more and offer her my pen instead, so she can draw a picture, but she will only reply in grunts, because today she is a baby polar bear. If I use her real name, she gets cross.

I unmute, talk through the next slide and quickly mute again as the baby polar bear has begun to crawl across my laptop.

I'm a contractor, so having work is a blessing right now. I help businesses to innovate and adapt, which is all very well when businesses are thinking three, four or five years ahead. But right now, most businesses are thinking in weeks, if not days. I know my work will dry up soon, so I've got to deliver what I can now. *Work from home unless you really can't,* goes the government advice. It's good advice. I'm all for it. It's just hard to execute, when at the same time you're supposed to be educating your children. There's one of me, two of them, and that's two full-time jobs, right there. And that's before you even think about cooking meals – endless meals! – to keep the children from getting in the state they're in now.

I once ran a marathon. Someone relayed to me some advice from Paula Radcliffe: *Don't think about the twenty-six miles. Just think about the mile ahead.* I'm taking that advice right now. I literally cannot deal with the idea that we might be doing this in September or beyond. I'm thinking about the next mile. Which, for me, means the hours between now and nine o'clock tonight, when I will be logging on to my laptop in peace, working out what actually happened on my calls, wiping the glitter from the keys, maybe even having a beer.

The double-job thing doesn't add up. I realise that now. At first, I thought I could be Super Woman and work 9 p.m. till 1 a.m., but then I quickly became so frazzled that I found myself shouting at the children for minor crimes like making a sandpit out of my stockpiled rice and drawing a picture with my mascara. I've been leaving them to their own devices a lot, so it's hardly a surprise when these things happen. So, no more 1 a.m. working. I just do what I can, when I can.

As for educating my girls . . . well, I've found muting the class WhatsApp group to be very good for my mental health. While other parents are helping their children to tell the time, bake crumble and construct Greek temples out of toilet rolls, I have effectively let mine go feral.

The three-year-old is now crawling, still baby polar bear-style, into the kitchen, while the five-year-old has gone suspiciously quiet.

I talk my client through the final slide, a sense of relief creeping up on me, although my mouse is still hovering on mute.

'We need to offer products that help our customers to look after the planet,' I say. 'Because it's not just up to individuals, it's about supply chains changing. It goes all the way to the top.'

I have a brief moment of clarity, enough freedom of thought to let my mind wander and question whether, 'when this is all over', as we keep saying, we'll do things differently. Will our panic over food make us think a little more about sustainable, locally sourced produce? Will negative oil prices prompt us to question its real value? Will the force of Mother Nature provoke a little more respect from humans around the world?

Closer to home, I've heard friends talk about how they are thinking of home educating their children. I can only imagine they're doing a better job than me.

I thank the participants on the call and sign off, shutting the laptop, ready to attempt some quality mother-and-daughter time. I find the five-year-old shut in her room, a little note slipped under the door that reads: 'SAY SOREY THEN I WILL COME OOT OF MY ROOM.' I brace myself, apologise, although I've lost track of what I'm apologising for, and go in for a cuddle.

I find the baby polar bear in the kitchen. She tells me she's making an omelette. She's cracked three eggs into a colander and is merrily adding milk. Eggy milk is all over the floor. I sigh. All in all, I have a lot to be thankful for.

Steve

A Priest's Chronicle

14 May 2020

More than before Covid-19, I am aware that I live and work in two very different worlds. I know that I'm very lucky: my wife and I share a small house on the edge of the Surrey Hills. It's a beautiful part of the country.

In what used to be normality, we passed much of our free time away from home. Nothing too exciting. We'd travel to see family or wander to places that piqued our interest. We knew there were lovely places around us, but we didn't really get to know our local area.

Being compelled to stay home, protect the NHS and save lives has meant we've become better acquainted with where we live. At the weekend, we walked a local stretch of the Black-water Valley and saw our first kingfisher. We baked lockdown loaves and sat in the garden with a glass of wine being gently hypnotised by the lazy wheel of a lonely red kite.

In the traffic-free quiet, home has been recovered as a place to *live* and to rejuvenate, and as I've not done for some time, to remember that my home world is a world full of living.

I'm doubly lucky, because I'm among those people who've been able to continue working. This gives me a measure of social connection and, as a hospice chaplain, my job gives me a sense of purpose that aids my mental wellbeing.

But continuing to work during the pandemic, I've become aware, more than ever before, of the contrast between home, as a place full of living, and work, as a place for dying; and aware too of the way that the pandemic has deepened and distorted the sadness that goes with dying.

Yesterday, I sat with a man and his daughter. He was around my age; she was about the age of my children. She and I were wrapped up in our PPE – aprons, gloves, goggles, surgical masks. And as her father was taking his last breaths, she was weeping the first of the many tears she will cry because the man who had always been there for her was slipping out of her life. Her tears were made all the more bitter by the restrictions the virus was putting on her visits – she was allowed little more than an hour a day.

This woman's sadness was not unique; similar scenes in similar rooms are played out around the building most days. But separation and isolation at this most poignant of times raises commonplace sadness to the level of tragedy.

Nor is her tragedy unique. Its replication and the feeling of impotence it compels intensify the dying and, for me, they sharpen the contrast I experience between being at home among the living and being at work among the dying.

More than that, they sharpen the increasing sense of disconnect that I have in speaking about those with whom I am at work, with those I am with when I am at home.

Lauren
Schools Closed, Exams Cancelled
01 May 2020

18 March 2020 was the day when my world as a Year 13 student fell apart. In the days leading up to it I had begged my parents to let me go to school, but I was struggling with severe asthma and it was too much of a risk. I was stuck at home, desperate for my lessons and desperate for my teachers, crestfallen and morose as I finished off the last of my revision materials for the summer exams.

And then on Wednesday it was announced that exams had been cancelled; truly my worst nightmare realised. I rang my aunt in inconsolable hysterics. I had spent my whole school career working as hard as I could, rarely going out and running between my lessons (usually in a paradoxical state of stressed enjoyment) – my school was a happy place for me. The stilts upon which I had balanced my life disintegrated beneath me and it felt like a sleep paralysis episode, with everything that I treasured made horrifyingly transparent and amorphous, and depressingly out of my control. The first week was hard; my mum is a headteacher, my dad is researching Covid-19 for his university and my aunt is a frontline GP, so I was deeply anxious, isolated from my friends, as well as still suffering badly with my asthma.

I emailed my teachers and as always, their support helped me to clear the lost fug that had settled over me. I enrolled in a free Open University course. I started painting. I slowly read through the two-foot stack of books that had been waiting patiently at my bedside for months. I asked anyone who would listen to play Scrabble with me. I began to teach myself early philosophy. I had an idea for a book and started to write.

Of course, those are the good days. Sometimes I feel overwhelmed, stranded, and I know that the only thing I will do is binge-watch *Game of Thrones* again or make a really amazing cheese toastie. But that's OK. When I moved my revision pile of books to my bookshelf in a tidying-up bout, I had to sit down and cry, because I knew what it signified. As it happens my last day of school was the thirteenth of March, when we had our school Book Day and I was the only year 13 to dress up (all in purple, as *The Color Purple*). I walked out of the gates without knowing it would be for ever.

I'm still scared, just like so many others out there, but now is the time to be brave. So today, that is what I choose.

Jo

As They Walk Down to the Sea

22 April 2020

This is the story of the end of my mum's life. She was eighty-nine, had dementia and breast cancer, and she had been living in a care home for two years. Her death was expected, a relief in some ways, but the circumstances were unprecedented and extraordinary – today's normality.

I last saw my mum on the fifteenth of March, visiting her in the care home with my ninety-year-old dad, as we always did on Sunday afternoons, for a cup of tea and a fig roll. My mum was always so pleased to see us, her face would light up like a child's, and she would nod along with our conversation, joining in here and there. She knew we loved her.

The care home closed to visitors two days later.

I had a call from a carer on the fifth of April to say that my mum had not been eating and hardly drinking for nearly a week. The care home called daily with updates, and by the seventh, a Tuesday, I asked whether we would be allowed to go and say goodbye. The manager was really unsure, but overnight she had a meeting with the staff involved, then spoke to Public Health England for advice. On Wednesday morning when I called, they said we could go in that afternoon, so my dad, brother and I went along. My poor dad cried all the way, saying he wouldn't be able to cope.

We all had our temperatures taken when we arrived at the home, and put on gowns and masks to walk through the corridors up to her room. When we went into her room, Mum didn't recognise us as our faces were covered and we had been told to keep our distance. I thought it was not going to go well.

But then the carer said that she was going to leave us there and we should lock the door behind her. She said once she had gone, we were free to do as we liked, as long as when we rung the bell to leave we were masked up again, with washed hands.

As soon as we took our masks off and went over to Mum, she knew we were her family and we had such a wonderful time together. She held our hands and my dad sat and brushed her hair, which she loved. She looked at him and said, 'I love you.'

After a while she became drowsy and closed her eyes, but continued listening to us talking to her.

We held hands and read the Celtic prayer, which made us all cry.

May the road rise up to meet you.
May the wind be always at your back.
May the sun shine warm upon your face; the
rains fall soft upon your fields
and until we meet again,
may God hold you in the palm of His hand.

In the week that followed, we lived in a strange limbo, waiting for the phone to ring but dreading the inevitable. I visited my dad every day, for socially distanced therapy in his garden. Nearly every day he cried, as he gradually came to terms with the realisation that he would never see his wife of sixty-five years again. The thought of her being alone during those last few days was unbearable. My mum has always been afraid of dying, and she also hated being alone. If my dad was away when I was a child, she would ask me to sleep in her bed, so that she wasn't on her own.

I am a teacher, and the phone call finally came as I was preparing the online lessons for my class, due to be sent out that afternoon. The carer I spoke to, who I know as a kind and gentle man, sounded weary and stressed. I didn't dare ask if anyone was with my mum when she died.

On the walk round to my dad's house, I received a text from my cousin to say that her ninety-seven-year-old mother, my mum's sister, was near the end of her life. She lived eighty miles away, and we hadn't seen her for a couple of years. Somehow the thought of my aunt dying too was a comfort, as I hoped they might be together again, hand in hand on Ramsgate seafront as they were as children.

Anyway, we told my dad, and spent the afternoon with him, talking about my mum, sharing our tears and memories. I called the doctor's surgery, where the registration of my mum's death was being processed, I called the care home to thank them, and to arrange for me to collect her possessions, and I called the funeral directors, who said they would call me back on Monday.

Over the weekend, my coping strategy was not to tell anyone if I could avoid it. Close family aside, I managed to reply briefly and with neutrality to friends' messages.

On Monday morning, I was due to 'meet' my class on Zoom to welcome them back to the summer term. Of course my headteacher said that I didn't have to do this in the circumstances, and had we been in school I would not have felt strong enough to go, but knowing how much the children would be looking forward to seeing their teacher made it necessary, while the barrier of the computer monitor made it possible.

Half an hour before Zooming, I heard from my cousin that my aunt had died earlier that morning.

During our Zoom Circle Time with screen-struck five- and six-year-olds, a surreal experience in itself, my phone kept whirring, with an unknown number. Returning the call at the end of my school session, it was the funeral directors.

I spoke to Richard, a kind and empathetic man. He gave us a date for my mum's funeral – 01 May

– and a choice of times on that day. 'Choose quickly,' he encouraged. 'Time slots are going fast.' I called the priest, who had a clear diary. I also thought I should check with my other brother, who would be driving from Stratford on the day. He answered my call saying that he was in a TEAMs meeting and could he call me back? 'No,' I explained, 'but you have twenty seconds to choose: timing for Mum's funeral – ten, one or four?'

The experience of my mum's end of life has, at times, felt like a black comedy, with layer upon layer of unbearable episodes building towards an excruciating climax.

Everything is so strange, so different, so unknown, including our feelings and reactions. Decisions that would normally be talked through and agonised over are arbitrary and reached in seconds. Feelings that are so deeply rooted and fundamentally human seem impossible to face but also easy to avoid amidst the practicalities of staying at home and social distancing. I still haven't told many friends about my mum's death, and I'm not sure when I will.

I have not listened to the news for over a week now, as everything seems to be focused around death rates in care homes. My mum will not be one of those statistics, as she died on the day she was ready to go. I can see her now, holding hands with her sister as they walk down to the sea.

Becky

Hospice Care

05 April 2020

I am a hospice doctor. In some ways my working day continues as usual. My hospital colleagues are able to postpone knee replacements and cataract operations, but my patients cannot delay dying from cancer, much as they'd like to.

On top of this, suddenly everyone wants a piece of me. Doctors less used to working with people at the end of life are asking for help in having difficult conversations about ceilings of care with patients who before Covid-19 we wouldn't have expected to die. We have developed guidelines to manage symptoms that these patients may experience as they die, knowing we might not be able to source the drugs we would usually use, or the kit to give them by injection as we would normally do.

I am so grateful that I have an amazing district-wide specialist palliative care team. We've always been pro-active about identifying the patients who we wouldn't be surprised if they died in the next few months or a year, and so have already had conversations about advance care planning and resuscitation status with many. But there are different conversations to be had with others – that under normal circumstances they might get escalated to critical care but just now that may not be an option.

I worry about my hospice. I may deliver care to NHS patients, but I am employed by a charity. We get some money from the NHS, but most comes from fundraising. And this has virtually dried up: our shops have shut; we've had to cancel the upcoming events we had planned. We've furloughed as many staff as possible and our fundraising team work tirelessly to come up with innovative ways of keeping the money coming in. My nephew has made NHS rainbow badges to sell on his street.

Another worry is staffing. A small hospice means a small pool of staff. As colleagues test positive, the pool gets smaller. For a while. Our senior management are donning uniforms and metaphorically rolling up their sleeves. At least we've got plenty of gloves and masks, but we had to put a plea on Facebook for eye protection as we only had two sets of safety glasses. And when I'm at home I'm sewing scrubs for my doctors. The first couple of sets were quite fun, but now it's getting tedious.

So, life is busy and days are long. But each day is a day nearer the end. And I hope one legacy will be a new appreciation of the importance of end of life care.

Nicola

Please Don't Clap for Me . . .

08 May 2020

It's Thursday. It's 8 p.m. I love the beautiful sound of our historic church bell resonating, faithfully rung marking the week as we celebrate our wonderful NHS and other frontline workers.

But please don't clap for me. Yes, I'm an NHS GP. Yes, I've offered to work overtime with Covid-19 patients. Yes, for the foreseeable future I'm hiding away from my husband – he's in a vulnerable group – as I practise strict social distancing in the spare room, complete with microwave, fridge and toaster loaned generously by strangers. Yes, in those early days, seemingly an eternity ago now, I was overwhelmed with daily updates – how do I spot the wood for the trees in the twenty-seven emails, all of which are important? – and yes, I'm naturally inflexible, and flexibility is in demand in the Covid Crisis as brave colleagues set up our new Hubs and Rainbow hospital services in unbelievable time . . .

But the Covid Lockdown hasn't been all bad. In fact, it's starting to suit me, I'm embarrassed to admit. Please don't clap for me.

So many are sick. Dying. Alone. Or wishing they were alone, unable to hide away from their abusive partner – no one claps for them. Or working from home, supposedly – juggling confused small children vying for attention. Serious job losses. Financial hardship. Struggling food banks. Inequalities hugely increased.

I, however, settle into my new normal – variety – grateful for corridor conferences that I realise are a luxury now; collaboration with neighbouring practices; the excitement and enthusiasm for our Rainbow hospital. Well-paid secure employment. Relieved, to be honest, to have an emptier diary. My violin in my bedroom. Things to keep me stimulated. And such magnificent sunshine, spring greenery, as during my daily permitted exercise I finally explore the countryside footpaths near us. New connections with the network of neighbours. Existing connections maintained with WhatsApp, Zoom, etc . . . I count my blessings.

Clap, yes, if you like, but I don't need your appreciation. I will be ringing my handbell for all our lowly carers, the truly frontline and heroic. For our humble shop workers, keeping us fed. For our teachers, exposed, grappling with impossible logistics ahead – as for so many, the future so unsure. For the bus drivers. For the abused, the suicidal, the hungry, the lonely, the grieving. For all the forgotten and lost.

Can I see a rainbow – of hope, of promise, of change – to esteem and honour and appreciate the lowly, the needy, to make our society more equal?

I celebrate you all. We are truly in this together. Thank you.

Seán

Lockdown Hubris

19 April 2020

The predominant sense of 'culture' once meant something that was grown in a petri dish. In our current period of coronavirus pandemic, culture is again framed biologically. In lockdown living, culture is symbolised for me by sourdough being cultivated in the fridge.

My days are now structured around a meal plan that I even enjoy drawing up. In the pre-coronavirus era, I cherished the chaos of my life. There wasn't much cooking, and when there was: well, I'd love picking up bits and pieces for dinner here and there, as a sort of postmodern hunter-gatherer – in the Tesco local around the corner, or in the little Sainsbury's on the way home from work. Now, my weekly highlight is the novelty of one big shop in Waitrose. In my early thirties, I've finally risen to the challenge of working out just how much I eat in a week and buying accordingly. If I were to have been accused of stockpiling at the start of lockdown, I would've pleaded domestic ignorance . . .

My relative state of happiness every other day has been thanks to taking up running. It surprised me how I became such a fitness fan overnight. I'm a lecturer for a living, and so I'm normally wedded to a life of the mind. My academic curiosity has shifted; for example, eighteenth-century socially critical idylls, which lightly but ironically depict the frustrations of domestic life, now resonate with me. Epicureanism, or the philosophy of bodily pleasures, is suddenly interesting. Ditto historical literature about garden grottos. But I can't concentrate on reading or writing all day at home.

And since I'm single, live alone, and now lead an all-the-more solitary life, running has become my coping strategy. A chance to interact with others, albeit from a distance. After getting shouted at by those who insisted on walking narrow paths three abreast in the middle of the day, I changed to 7 a.m. outings for my daily release from house arrest. I was adopted into the elite group of early risers, who smile in solidarity.

We are those who are sovereign over a disciplined, daily routine. I began to feel smug, confident that I'd emerge from lockdown more energetic, more organised, and more comfortable with my own company.

On Saturday, my new world came crashing down. I'm now more housebound than before. Oh no, mercifully I haven't contracted corona-virus. I merely sprained an ankle. Nevertheless, spending my mornings with a bag of frozen peas, a dose of self-pity, and googling how to embrace mindfulness, I've had to scale back my grand plan to emerge from this stay-at-home life as super-fit or a domestic god. (Last week I also managed to scald myself cooking pasta). The Romantic cliché that in a crisis is born creativity, and a stronger self? I've consigned that to the history books. So this weekend, I waved goodbye to my lockdown hubris.

My body has its limits. So too does my ability, and enthusiasm, to reinvent myself.

Pete

Family Bonds

01 May 2020

Life in lockdown feels strangely familiar. Lots of people have observed how it's like the period between Christmas and New Year. Days of the week have become irrelevant and wearing pyjamas 24/7 is socially acceptable. But I'm also reminded of different times, the weeks after our two sons arrived in our family.

My husband and I are proud dads to two wonderful boys through adoption. When you adopt a child, you are told to have a few weeks when you stay home and see no-one. Extended family are instructed to stay away. Excited friends are warned that they must be patient. You should go out only when it's essential. Sound familiar?

We've had these periods of isolation twice and they were both tough. Your life is changing dramatically and you have to adapt to new roles and schedules. You fear nothing is ever going to be the same again and you're sure that you're getting everything wrong. You are bored and long for variety and stimulation. Most of all you miss your friends and family and crave familiar faces to offer advice and tell you everything is going to be all right. Again, sound familiar?

We all know it takes a village to raise a child. I appreciate over-eager relatives and endless streams of visitors can be difficult to manage but there's something strange about new parents finding their feet on their own, separated from everyone they know and love.

And yet, those periods of family lockdowns were not just helpful, they were essential. Without the support of genetic links and hormonal surges, we relied on time and endless, caring tasks to build the bonds of love between parent and child. Without us even noticing it, relationships within our family were transformed simply by having time, just with each other. We fell utterly in love with children who were once strangers.

It is my hope that lots of other families might emerge from this period of national lockdown similarly strengthened. It won't be true for all, especially those who do not feel safe in their homes. But for many, having faced this extraordinary time as households, alone but together, it might mean that the bonds of family feel more powerful than ever.

Sarah

When Your Animal is Sick

08 May 20

On Monday my husband took our little cat Squeak to the vet. The combined effect of lockdown, furloughing and social distancing mean that the practice is working with minimum manpower, and appointments are hard to obtain and reserved for emergencies only.

The procedures are precise; you arrive in the car park at your pre-arranged time and alert the vet to your presence. The box containing the pet is left on the step and, once you have retreated the accepted distance, the vet opens the door and collects your much-loved bundle. The initial assessment, diagnosis and discussion of options and costs have taken place by phone prior to the carpark rendezvous. Any face-to-face communication is sparse . . . and loud, if it is to traverse the physical distance.

Squeak's condition was worse than expected and required additional discussions between surgery and carpark about the necessity of more procedures. And so time passed. The next human arrived with his canine friend in a box. The man sat on the ground talking gently to his dog as they waited.

Squeak came home on a warm day and roamed around our garden. That night she slept in the bottom of our wardrobe, a place she loved. The next day her condition deteriorated and after touring all her favourite sunny spots, as the late afternoon sun cooled, she came in and gently died. Normally my work takes me away from home in the morning and back by mid-evening. Now, with Covid-19, I am working from home. There are surely not many joys to be derived from the current situation but for me, one of the unexpected graces is that I was there and able to soothe her, care for her, to share those last few days and hours with the beautiful creature who had shared with me the ups and downs of the last fifteen years.

Yet this will not be everyone's experience and I will be eternally grateful that I managed to avoid the fate of the man in the vet's carpark. As my husband prepared to drive away, he saw the vet stop briefly outside the practice before disappearing behind a firmly shut door and returning with the man's beloved companion; and he saw the man nod quietly in answer to her question, 'Do you want the body back?'

Gabriella

Superpower

05 May 2020

'Nope!'

This is the common answer I now hear from my four-year-old daughter. After more than six weeks of lockdown she rejects any activity I suggest. Above all, she does not like school work.

'Counting game?'

'Nope!'

'Painting?'

'Nope!'

'Reading book?'

'I am never, ever reading again.'

I venture: 'How about we learn just one phonics sound?'

She picks up her yellow exercise book – the one the school gave us before it closed. I feel a flutter of hope that she's going to say yes. But she slips it into a kitchen cupboard when she thinks I'm not looking.

'Mummy, my yellow book is invisible,' she announces.

I'm not surprised she's had enough. Our home-schooling environment is far from ideal. Every time I try to teach, her baby brother shouts for attention from his highchair. I wave a toy at him with one hand and try to overcome the noise. Meanwhile their two-year-old sister makes a dash for the potty and yells: 'Mummy! Wipe my botty!' My husband is working full time, so uninter-rupted minutes are gold dust.

It's reassuring that my mum friends say their children have grown similarly disengaged. On our reception class WhatApp group one writes: 'Mine has spent the day under a table dressed as a Power Ranger.' Another: 'He's cramming epi-sodes of *Andy's Dinosaur Adventures*.'

Missing her friends is part of the problem and staying in touch has proved challenging. Zoom chats are anathema. It's completely unnatural for children her age to sit and converse. They like to run alongside each other, sharing toys and games.

If we happen across a friend in real life on our daily bike ride, they stare at each other, two metres apart, silent. It's heartbreaking.

Is the answer returning to school? I'm not so worried about her formal education – she will learn to read and write eventually. But I'm desperate for her to have her normal life back. Otherwise, her 'nope!' attitude may become ingrained – perhaps forever.

Although science shows children suffer least, it feels as though we're sending our little people to the frontline. Coronavirus couldn't care less about our economy. And if my husband and I get sick, how will we care for our trio?

My daughter's schoolwork is currently super-heroes-themed. I ask her: 'Would you like a superpower that would make the virus go away?' Finally, she answers: 'Yes.'

Hilary

Tea and Toast

02 May 2020

'Would you like a cup of tea and a piece of toast, love?' the nurse asked quietly.

It was the most comforting question I could have been asked. My world was spinning. I was exhausted and something so familiar in the midst of it all helped me get my bearings and prepare for what was to come.

It was six days since I had received a phone call one evening in my home in Canada. 'Your father has had a fall and has been taken to hospital in an ambulance.' My father was ninety-six years old and had stumbled with his walker. The moment I had dreaded and anticipated for so long was here.

'He is very poorly,' the doctor told me, taking time out of her busy hospital shift to speak to me on WhatsApp and let me see him.

There he was like a fallen old oak tree, lying in the bed in his hospital gown, unable to hear me because he had been completely deaf for years. I had always promised him, 'If you are taken to hospital, I will be on the next plane.'

What seemed impossible in the midst of the Covid-19 crisis, somehow became possible. I had a seat on a plane that same evening. That beautiful doctor again took the time during her shift to meet me at the hospital entrance and take me to his ward. He was classified as 'End of Life' and so I was allowed to be there. I was in the hospital beside his bed within twenty-four hours of leaving home, and the minute I walked in he said, 'I feel safe now you are here.'

I spent the next five days visiting him every day, hearing the same words, 'I feel safe now you are here. Are you leaving tomorrow?' I constantly reassured him I was not.

The hospital was a flurry of activity, machines, masks and ventilators, and PPE put on and off every time a nurse entered and left the ward. My father was tested for Covid-19 but the results never came. He had a heart attack and there was nothing they could do for him.

It is not what nurses and doctors do medically that has the greatest impact; it is their kindness.

It is this kindness to which I want to pay tribute. Thank you to the nurse who found out my dad would eat nothing but custard and made sure he had it every day. Thank you to the nurse who found me a charger for my phone so my father could say goodbye on WhatsApp to his family in Canada and his great grandchildren in Africa.

Thank you to the doctor who said, 'I want to hug you, but I can't, so I will just touch your arm.'

Thank you to the nurse who said, 'Would you like a cup of tea and a piece of toast, love?' taking me into a quiet room and helping me gain my strength to go back to his bedside, where I had been holding his hand for eight hours, to hold it just a little longer until he took his last breath.

In the midst of all your medical expertise, it is your kindness, the nurses and doctors on Ward 37, that I will never forget.

Thomas (age 14)
The Joys of Bellringing

01 May 2020

Hello, my name is Thomas and I'm fourteen years old. I'm on the autism spectrum, and I find it hard to make friends. Since 2017 I've been learning how to ring church bells. Bell ringing has changed my life: I've made new friends, and bell ringers have been extremely kind, supportive and helpful. Bellringing helps me relax and focus, and it takes my feelings away when I feel sad and upset. I enjoy bellringing because of how it's made me change as a person. When I first heard the sound of bells, it made me feel happy, joyful and excited, and when I started, I just couldn't stop. I visit lots of bell towers and it's really fun editing the bellringing videos for YouTube. I've made so many friends and hopefully will make more in the future. For me, bellringing has been a life-changing hobby.

From mid-March all bellringing was cancelled. I was really upset. I felt empty, heartbroken, sad and lost. I can't describe it.

Since then I've been keeping busy, because we have a discord server that keeps my bellringing friends and me connected and entertained. During these uncertain times, I've been learning bellringing methods on ringing room, a virtual ringing website where you ring church bells on the computer, such as plain bob minor. I've also been planning which church towers to visit after lockdown finishes, as well as seeing what I can do to make my YouTube channel videos better. I watch other people's bellringing videos to inspire me.

I do some school work and make a plan of my day. The Joe Wicks exercise is a very good resource, because it makes me stronger and fitter. These days the days go past rapidly, which is good. I like to talk to my cat sometimes and that helps me feel better.

I am sad that people are dying of coronavirus. We are supposed to be over the peak so hopefully we'll be out of lockdown soon. I thank the NHS for helping so many patients over the past weeks.

I am really grateful they are doing this not only because I want to go back to bellringing again, but because they are doing the best they can and being caring. I applaud that.

Geraldine

Rathlin Lockdown

14 May 2020

Mostly the weather has been kind. God tempering the wind to the shorn lamb and all that. I have been locked down in a very heaven. A small island of total peace and tranquillity. Last evening there were eighteen hares, count 'em, lolling in the field above; at the shore, there were eider ducks courting, and seals on the rocks soaking in the last of the sun; scarlet pimpernel still awake by the path; fat, furry mullein leaves thrusting, so many dog violets this year, tiny vibrant blue stars of gentian, early purple orchids, although not yet on the Chapel Brae. A floral fanfare for the spring. I am getting good at walking on the pebbles again, and I lift little white stones to make neat borders around my flower beds and pocket limpet shells to scatter in my own octopus's garden. Shipwrecked in paradise while others suffer, I feel guilty.

I am lonely for friends and family, but living here I often am. After decades of visiting and seven years' residence, I am still very much a 'blow-in'. In a long life of wandering I never landed in a place before where I did not find my tribe and forge enduring friendships. I have a connection to the land itself, a deep affinity with its basalt breaking through peaty soil, its bogs, heather and bracken, its salt-laden, wicked north-west winds. I never forgot my first visit, with my mother, more than fifty years ago. We came in a sea-tossed open boat, walked thigh-deep through lush wet grass to the East Lighthouse, had tea with her friend, tomato sandwiches cut into triangles and Marie biscuits. Sea voyages make you hungry.

Much later Rathlin called me back to find her small, lonely harbours, the wall-steads of abandoned clachans and a dark and eerie lough, as deep as the cliffs are high, with a standing stone nearby that lends you her magic. I lived another life here; every discovery is more a recognition than a novelty: the cairns, old mills, boat shelters built for curraghs, wrinkles on the hillside where barley and potatoes once grew. The past is everywhere and it murmurs to me all the time, tells me stories. I have been given time to listen.

An island reminds you that control is an illusion. Wind and tide decide if a boat will travel and mere mortals must change their plans, for more powerful forces are at play. We here are better equipped for these strange times, better at wait and see and better at turning to the next task at hand. Blessed indeed.

Naomi

How to be Present

08 May 2020

Our eight-year-old son Conrad has Lowe Syndrome, a very rare condition which includes him being globally delayed. He is not aware of Covid-19 and I don't think he is aware of lockdown either as he is very much in the present and seems blissfully unaware. This has been a time of deep connection with him for us. He needs twenty-four-hour support and care. Prior to lockdown he went to a specialist school during the day, and a few days a week we would have help from 'enablers' while I finished work, popped out for a swim, or took his brother and sister for a walk or to football or climbing sessions. Usually life is busy for us and, like many in the world, we have had to slow right down and be with what is immediately in front of us.

Conrad finds the most simple things a huge joy – I helped him climb onto a bed a couple of days ago and he said 'light on, please' and as the overhead light turned on and glowed, he belly laughed so much his body shook. Yesterday his sister and I wandered up into the field with him and he helped us give pellets to the chickens – he found great pleasure in the sensation of feeling the pellets in his hands and slowly dropping them onto the ground as chickens gathered around him. I was kneeling close by and I saw his older sister wipe a tear of joy from her eye as she watched him, proud, as he at times has been sensory averse and found something like dry chicken food really unpleasant to touch.

He reminds us to be young and playful. His older brother will play games of hide and seek that involve hiding under a blanket somewhere nearby and calling Conrad to 'come and find me', and I watch on as they laugh together, Conrad stamping his feet and swinging his arms – his way of expressing delight and excitement.

In the May sunshine he sits and throws stones into an upturned metal dustbin lid that he calls teapot and he says 'Mummy turn'. I take my turn too, enjoying the sounds and his joy as I throw the stones with speed and vigour, as I know it will make him laugh.

Later on that day we get a food delivery and when the driver leaves the van engine running, I hear a cross voice saying 'no school bus' – and so I realise he does remember things from before.

These are the parts I want to remember, so when moments with him are challenging I remind myself that I won't get this time back. Even if we have future periods of lockdown, they won't feel the same as the first. We are seven or even eight weeks into this current lockdown and on my non-work days there is a feeling of spaciousness, with no racing against the clock or any of the usual distractions, and I am actually present with him and I realise I haven't experienced this for many years.

Marjan

Singing to a Constantly Changing Key

01 May 2020

'I have told the carers that I want to see a doctor,' she told me. They asked what the reason was and 'I don't want to go on any more' had been her answer. We were about a week into the coronavirus lockdown. As my mother lives in a large institution for fragile old people, the doors were now locked against all visitors. The only joy in her life – the small glimpses of the outside world – had been taken away. To be kept alive for what, she wonders. She has been ready to die for some time now.

A few days into the lockdown she told me she was at the end of her tether. I could tell from the tone of her voice the moment she answered the telephone. Nervous. Terse. The staff are worried she is obsessed with the coronavirus crisis, as she seems to be following developments on her large loud TV screen incessantly. We wonder what else she is supposed to do; she is, aged ninety-four, still an intelligent woman interested in current affairs, politics and philosophy. She has always preferred to live in the here and now and never sought to find a means of escape in the form of a film or show.

Luckily this morning I have come prepared. As I had been struggling to find something to talk about on my twice-daily calls, I have armed myself with some Dutch poetry anthologies and books of songs. Do you want a song or a poem? I ask her. A poem! She shouts resolutely.

I read the oldest written Dutch poem kept in the Bodleian library. It is a monk's utterance in the margin of a page in Latin; he notices how the birds are starting to build their nests. 'Except you and me. What are we waiting for?' he asks.

Her mood lifts as we talk about the poem and think about the monk, writing, alone in his cell. It doesn't escape us that she is like him, alone with her thoughts in her cell.

Death is a frequent theme in the poems we read. Where did you find that one? She asks. In an anthology by a well-known Dutch poet, I remind her, and so we read his commentary. Some days she is deeply engaged and interested; at other times she will say: I don't get it; it doesn't do anything for me. And then she accuses me: you have the wrong idea about me; you think that I am intelligent! Well, I am not. You had better stop with these poems. No! I don't want another one!

And so we are back to: is the sun shining? (It is where she is, but not where I am. You see? You should've stayed here!) Did somebody come to take her outside in her wheelchair? (Making the day tolerable). Did she sleep? 'I have nothing else to tell you,' she says, never thinking to ask if anything of interest may have occurred in my life.

Today I sing for her. It is tricky because I hear the delayed echo of my voice in her especially-adapted-for-hard-of-hearing-seniors telephone. But I am strong and used to ignoring the discordant voice in my ear. That discordant voice I have grown up with is hers. She, who loves to sing, despite not being able to tell one note from another. She sings to a constantly changing key, somewhere up and somewhere down again. But her inability to keep in tune has never once taken away her enjoyment of singing, except when at school she was told to put her voice on mute during singing lessons. And so now, for my sister and me, it is the go-to place when we have run out of things to say and want to help her get through the day.

Maia Simona (age 14)
Nothing New

10 June 2020

For me, lockdown is nothing new. I have had chronic fatigue syndrome for around four years, ever since I was ten, and I'm used to the solitude, to the inability to go outside, to the overwhelming fear of nothing changing and work piling on top of me. So I've got myself under control. I wake up at 6.30 a.m. and read for half an hour (or whenever my mum tells me it's breakfast). I stack fruit and granola on top of my yoghurt and eat with my mum and brother. After I've had breakfast, I change into some shorts and a T-shirt to do PE with Joe. Over lockdown, I've managed to do half an hour of PE with Joe every day. It's amazing – I've not managed to do sports since I was ten! I can feel myself getting stronger every time I do it, which is the most incredible feeling. I start school the second I've finished PE with Joe (around 8.30 a.m.) and follow my school timetable. Each day, I have three hour-long lessons, all before lunch. I have one class on Microsoft Teams, with my maths teacher: our maths set are the guinea pigs of the school, as the teachers try to figure out what works. My work ethic is strong so I can spend the afternoon reading and resting. At 3.30 p.m., I go for a walk with my mum and brother around the park. We usually bring a snack or buy a lolly. I've developed a deep appreciation for nature over lockdown. While everything else is a chaotic inferno, the birds keep singing, the trees keep swaying and the sun keeps beaming (most of the time). When we get back, I call my best friend. We've known each other since we were three and, although we've drifted in and out of contact, we're now closer than ever. After a good chat, I help my mum with dinner and practise my Danish with her. I'd really recommend learning a language you've always wanted to improve on: it's a great distraction and you feel as though you're doing something productive. After dinner (spaghetti is my favourite), I sink into the fantasy of my book's pages and am whisked away from the coronavirus. This time is so frightening, especially for young people. We have Brexit, racism, global warming and now a pandemic to worry about. But reading transports me away from it all and, although it's just fiction, it keeps me sane. I turn off the lights at 9.30 p.m., as I do each and every night. This routine is a definite upgrade from the old one when I couldn't get out of bed or even hold a book. So, really, I am extremely grateful.

Lawrence

A New Unwanted Partner

01 May 2020

The coronavirus pandemic has presented me with a new unwanted partner – a deep and monstrous anxiety that gnaws away at my life-blood day and night.

I am not anxious for myself in purely coronavirus terms. There is even much about the lockdown that I enjoy. My anxiety is for my son, in lockdown in London 200 miles away. In that sense I am no different to thousands of other parents. Except my son has a brain tumour. To the naked eye he is a fit and healthy young man living his life to the full. But his brain tumour makes him different. And it makes our father–son relationship different too.

Since his diagnosis two years ago, we have met up every week to check in with each other, provide mutual support and generally keep ourselves on an even keel. Coronavirus has snatched this away from us and left us trying to stay emotionally connected through a virtual world. It is all we have and so we use it, but it doesn't work. I need to see my son, touch him, and look deep into his eyes to read his thoughts and assess his mood and mental health.

My son was supposed to have his six-month scan today. It was cancelled. He was told that due to coronavirus pressures on the NHS he won't have another one for a further six months – a full year since his last one. This has caused my son profound distress and yet I can't get to him to help him through this horrendous situation.

For the first time since my son's diagnosis I am experiencing a hot and livid anger. I absolutely know that getting on top of the coronavirus pandemic is crucial for all of us. But why has the government allowed the capacity in the NHS to become so depleted that it is unable to carry out other urgent treatments? Why is a coronavirus patient given priority over my son and others like him? Why am I even having to speak these dreadful words?

The coronavirus will pass. My son's brain tumour will not. In the meantime my new invisible and malign partner gets bigger by the day and causes far more distress than the virus that triggered it.

Kaye

A Perpetual Knot of Guilt

16 May 2020

Wednesday 25 March 2020 will forever be a memorable date. It was my husband Mark's forty-second birthday, celebrated with a dense sponge cake baked with the wrong type of flour and enthusiastically decorated by our three-year-old daughter and five-year-old son, using leftover Milk Tray from my thirty-eighth birthday, from the previous week. Following the obligatory candles, a well-practised, due to hand washing, rendition of 'Happy Birthday' and a good spray of child-saliva on the Milk Tray, I packed a large suitcase with three months' worth of comfortable clothes and said my goodbyes to my little family.

You see, I am an immuno-supressed kidney transplant recipient, saved from a life of dialysis ten years ago by my wonderful, selfless dad. This means that I fall into the 'extremely vulnerable' category and government advice is to 'shield' for at least twelve weeks. I am fortunate in that my parents have a holiday cottage only forty minutes' drive from home, so, with a heavy heart and photos of my children, crudely but delightfully displayed in hand-decorated frames made for Mothers' Day, I left home and am now on week seven of solitary isolation in a holiday cottage neighbouring my parents' house.

Unfortunately, emergency surgery in August last year led to the failure of my kidney transplant, but this does at least give me a reason to leave the house three times a week: I travel back to my home town and receive four hours of dialysis treatment every other evening. I have a lot to be grateful for – the very fact that this life-saving treatment is available – and the change of lifestyle from busy mum and assistant headteacher in a secondary school to splendid isolation has given me plenty of time to keep circumstances in perspective and maintain my 'attitude of gratitude'. I am grateful for the NHS staff who run the unit. I am grateful to my parents for putting me up and filling my fridge. I am grateful for my husband who has taken on sole child-care responsibilities as well as running our home and working full time. I am grateful to my friends for their virtual checking up and cheering up. And I am so proud of my children who have proven themselves to be more resilient, independent and adaptable than I had given them credit for.

Yes, at times it's excruciatingly painful being away from my family. Watching the children play, reading them bedtime stories and learning about their day via video call is no substitute for the desperate cuddles of five- and three-year-old children who sometimes, just need their mum. I have a perpetual knot of guilt in my stomach. But being apart for twelve weeks is a small price to pay, if the alternative is being apart forever.

Liz

Hand to My Heart, Arm Outstretched

07 May 2020

She is leaning against the gatepost waiting for me. I watch her as I approach, and I know she's wondering when I will stop to maintain the safe distance between us. For over thirty-two years I've learned to read every flicker of emotion in her face, for when her disability robs her of language.

I stop two and half metres away. 'Hi,' I say. She smiles back, uncertain how to proceed with this new normality that leaves an empty space where her hug should be. I sign 'I love you' in Makaton – hand to my heart, arm outstretched, and she replies. I'm still grateful to this wonderful sign language that's helped us communicate, despite the barriers that Down's Syndrome has placed in her path.

I put a small plastic bag on the ground and step back, I've brought some hand gel that, incredibly, I've managed to find – it feels like some illegal drugs deal. While she's putting it in her backpack I look down the drive to the supported flats where she lives and see Jenny, the house manager, in the office window talking on the phone. It's still strange to see her in face mask and gloves, there's a sudden sense of the risk that she, and every other care worker, is taking and I feel huge gratitude.

Hannah loves living here, she loves her independence. But the risk of infection is a complex issue for her, as she has OCD – obsessive compulsive disorder – with a phobia of germs. After all those months of being told she doesn't need to wash her hands so much and that germs have never hurt her, she is now being told all that has changed. I've watched a shadow of confusion pass over her face, and her hands become raw and cracked.

She will go on for her shopping and I'll turn back home, so we walk down the hill together. That's difficult on a narrow pavement, so I walk in front of her, backwards, so we can still talk. It becomes a game where she steers me away from walls or bins. I make a play of getting snagged in a bush and we laugh. The distance between us feels less.

At the bottom of the hill I remind her not to touch her face or stand too close to anyone at the checkout, and she says, 'Mum, I know!' I let it go, say goodbye and start to walk up my hill. I look back across the wide, empty road between us, she puts her hand on her heart and stretches out her arm to me, turns towards the shops and is gone.

Tom

I'd Like to Wake Up Now

30 April 2020

I'm halfway into my second nightshift and I'm tired. I tell my colleagues it's because my toddler woke me up but this is only half true. The reality is that I cannot stop thinking about the coronavirus. My brain hums with panic and I can't drift off. I know I should try to let it go; searching the news for updates, numbers and graphs is only adding to my anxiety. It pervades every corner of my life.

I am a senior paediatric registrar. Before the crisis changed everything, I was due to complete my training and become a consultant in September of this year. This, like so much else, is now uncertain. Being a paediatrician with two small children of my own, I can't seem to be able to escape talking about, thinking about or planning around the virus. It seeps in to every facet of my professional, family and personal life. It feels like a weight, hovering just above my head and clouding my thoughts and vision.

At work, the topic is discussed endlessly. Not just in the swapping of rumours and during coffee breaks but in hastily convened meetings, Q&As, training sessions, ward rounds. No one quite knows what the most up-to-date guidelines or recommendations are. They seem to change daily. Fact and hearsay become jumbled and absorbed in a disorientating blur of half understood information.

At home my phone and email ping constantly with messages from colleagues and posts to the workplace group chat: videos of seminars, articles, comparisons of epidemic curves across different countries (they're almost all the same). Family and friends are desperate to connect: some for information and reassurance I can't give, some because they are shut away from physical contact with their loved ones. Aside from my wife and our children, I haven't seen my family in weeks. I start to wonder if my daughters, one of whom is just a month old, will ever be held by their grandparents again. In ten years' time will I be telling them to be careful with that picture, as it's the only one we have of them both with their grandfather? Being under two, neither of them understands the impact the virus is having on our lives but I think daily about what it will have on theirs: such a range of possibilities, many of which don't bear thinking about.

At night the hospital is empty. At the moment, the paediatric ward is unusually quiet. It makes me wonder where all the genuinely sick children who normally fill the beds at this time of year have gone. But it also gives me and my colleagues time to sit and stew in our anxiety. It would be better if we were busier. The double doors at the entrance to the ward look out onto the corridor between ITU and the ambulance bay. Intermittently the night-time silence is broken by the crash of a trolley rumbling down the corridor, flanked by staff in visors and face masks warning others to keep their distance. I try not to look at the occupants of the beds. Doing so might make it seem too human, too close to home. Better to focus on the peripheries and keep it all as something otherworldly. After a few seconds the flash of voices and urgency dies down and the hallway is empty again. I wonder if it's safe to go out in the hallway, or if the virus still lingers in the air and on the walls, the polished green hospital floor.

In my sleep-deprived state, I start to wonder, in a very real sense, whether this could all be a dream. The familiar sense of creeping dread and queasy unreality of an anxiety dream or nightmare linger behind me, following me wherever I go. Combined with sleep deprivation in a dingy back-room doctors' office at 2 a.m., the distinction between reality and nightmare genuinely isn't so clear.

Most of all, I am scared. I'm not the only one. I know this for certain, although it's rarely given voice by my colleagues lest giving name to it would make it stronger. It's not lost on any of us, the risks involved with being at work. In some ways, I am lucky. I am relatively protected on my paediatric ward and unlikely to be needed at the front line proper in adult ITU or acute medicine. I often feel ashamed and cowardly at myself for the relief I feel at this. Even so, part of me wants to run and quit. Yet another part of me wants to volunteer to work on those already overcrowded adult wards, to stand up and face it head on, almost as if in confrontation the power it has over me would diminish. But I know I won't do this.

The virus follows me home. Both literally and figuratively. I can't escape thinking about it as I commute back and forth on the tube. Where should I stand? What shouldn't I touch? Who should I avoid? When I reach my front door I must wash my hands and strip off my clothes before I can greet my family or I risk infecting them. I envy my oldest daughter. Too young to appreciate the worry shouldered by all of us. Although I am certain she can feel the tension and it manifests in tantrums and poor sleep.

I think about what it will be like on the other side when it's all over. I wonder if we will ever get there. I think for a moment about how relieved everyone will be but then realise that it won't be the same. All of us will be changed forever by this experience in a way that nothing in recent history has changed us before. I can only hope that some good will come out of it all. At the moment, it's hard to see what that might be.

I'm not prone to worry. I get on with things. I'm resilient. Tonight, though, I'm finding it hard to get on. Earlier today, my mother asked me if I was stressed and I said I was okay. But actually yes, I'm stressed. And there are others that have it much worse than me. And this is just the beginning.

I'd like to wake up now.

Lisa

Through My Phone

24 April 2020

My unlikely but constant companion through this Covid-19 experience has been my phone. By my side, wrapped and sealed in the cellophane bag usually used to put little vials of blood on their way from the ward to the lab for testing. It's been my companion throughout, not offering any advice or comfort to me, just witnessing. My phone has seen and heard things it never has before, and is unlikely ever to see again, certainly with the relentless frequency that it has done in recent weeks. In the absence of an NHS mobile or tablet on the ward, my phone has been placed next to an old lady's ear, on her pillow as she drifts into unconsciousness, breathing with shallow, irregular gasps, with hopes and promises from her daughter, hoping that her mum will be able to hear her final words of love, even though she can't be there to say them. Its speakerphone plays the voice of her ten-year-old granddaughter tearfully telling her that she wants her to come home to read to her again one day soon.

Its camera has facetimed the lovely man in Room 10 with his elderly wife and grown-up children, gathered in their living room, faces filling the small pocket-sized screen, grandchildren on more screens within screens who cannot be there with their parents because of the lockdown. Thanking him for being such a wonderful dad and granddad, telling him that they love him, and to sleep, now.

Its speakers have played favourite songs; Elvis albums and jazz compilations, songs that families have suggested will provide comfort in those last hours of life. It has been there with me and my patients, who have never seen my face, to alleviate our shared distress and distract from the sound of laboured breaths. Often abandoned without me, remaining in patients' rooms, an offering of humanity as I am called to assess a new or deteriorating patient. My phone has been my portal to my colleagues throughout these days. Many of whom I do not know because I am new to this hospital and just a number on the rota, and whose full faces I rarely see. The hospital now on its emergency Covid-19 rota has been run by WhatsApp groups, with the old bleep system, inadequate at the best of times, now almost obsolete. Doctors communicate between teams, shifts and zones; for endocrinology advice from a senior or specialist when sodiums are low, or delirium management needs expert advice and when food, kindly cooked by volunteers and community groups has arrived in the doctors' mess.

On my phone are weekly pictures of property bags of the dead, piled up in the store room waiting for collection by the porters, my own death figures captured weekly in a macabre picture. Each bag representing a person I cared for, my handwriting in their notes documenting my attempts to save them, and eventually, to keep them comfortable when alive, to be followed by my handwriting on certificates after their death. My phone's home screen that once proudly championed the beaming smiles and silliness of my young sons' faces is now a generic photograph, previously stored in its factory settings. The phone's torch light has proved useful for confirming deaths in the absence of pen torches on the ward. Pupils fixed and dilated. The faces of my beautiful smiling children in the forefront of my view on the phone screen, merged with the torchlight reflected in the dead man's eyes before me in real life – pupils fixed and dilated – a visceral reminder of a separate world that I have inhabited over these weeks, associated with an intense pang of guilt that I had in that moment somehow exposed my babies to this world that I should be protecting them from.

The final role my phone has played during the coronavirus pandemic has been when I am lying in bed at night, unable to sleep or waking from vivid dreams. My phone distracts me, although as I trail mindlessly through social media, I try my best to avoid any news – I don't want to be consumed by any bigger picture, for fear of being overwhelmed. Content and able to cope with my micro-level involvement with this pandemic, with my phone beside me that has allowed me both to stay connected and to disconnect. It's been my lifeline and without it, I think we would have all been lost.

Esther

Confessions of a Keyworker

19 June 2020

In years to come people will share tales of their lockdown life. Families will joke about the trials of being stuck at home, how they tried to home school, how the weather was unreal. The TV shows will mention Joe Wicks's PE lessons, will talk about a shared experience, how the nation went through it together. None of that will resonate for me as that hasn't been my lockdown; my Covid-19 life.

As a *key worker* life has gone on. I get up every morning and go to work. One daughter has gone to school, one to nursery. We escape the days on end at home, the struggle of the same four walls. And I am both grateful for it and sad.

Despite being an NHS manager, not a front-line worker, when lockdown begins my manager issues me with a letter telling those that need to know that I am 'essential to the fight against

Covid'. Every time I drop my daughter off at school, they thank me for all I am doing. I feel like a fraud.

Going to work makes me feel disconnected from friends and family. My WhatsApp groups are filled with tips on home schooling and tales about lockdown life. There is a shared experience in lockdown and it feels, to me who isn't really locked down, like camaraderie. I cannot participate. Life is very different, but also, for us, so very much the same. My friends thank me for all I am doing. I secretly think they have it harder.

My overwhelming feeling throughout it all is guilt. Social media shows me friends teaching children, going for walks, reconnecting as families. It may be lies, but it makes me feel terrible. The school sets work for home I don't even look at. Although my daughter is physically in school, the school repeatedly tells me it is childcare provision, not education. I worry she is slipping behind.

My youngest's nursery tells us, after just two weeks of lockdown, it has to close. My daughter can go to another nursery a few miles away. It is a nursery I have never seen, nursery workers I have never met. I take her and leave her at the door in the arms of a woman I don't know the name of. I cannot go into the nursery because, well, Covid. I cry the whole way to work.

Friends worry about sending children back to school and I say nothing, as my children have never left.

It turns out that, like Covid-19, guilt can come in waves.

Simon

Lockdown Exercise

29 April 2020

I can't go swimming with Wycombe Masters any more and this gives me the problem of how I can replace my three sessions a week while stuck at home.

Thirty-minute live Facebook broadcasts at 6.30 a.m. from Arabella the physical trainer who runs the Monday night circuit class in the Village Hall, come to my rescue. I slide out of bed down to the living room hoping that there won't be any noisy running on the spot permeating the ceiling and waking my REM land-of-nod wife. My phone, delicately nestled against a cushion on the chair, charging cable snaked from the plug, lights up. Arabella starts the session, 'Usual format, sign in and let me know you're here.' I've been dreaming of posting a one-way one-liner that invokes a response ahead of the other participants. Arabella doesn't know how much pondering it has taken, as she tries to avoid saying 'so' each time a new exercise is introduced. Fourteen this morning.

I'm about to get on the floor for crunches and through the window I spy a rat running by, fat from eating the bird food that's been spat out by the blue tits; fussy buggers wanting something tastier. Now on my back and squeeze, squeeze, squeezing, I notice a painted edge of the lampshade. Last year's fit of unfit DIY. And that bracket holding up the curtain rail is completely skewiff. The thin, purple exercise mat is shredding at the edge, pieces of poly-something apparently, absolutely, utterly, selfishly destroying yesterday's hoovering of the living room.

Arabella floored me in her 'Looking After Your Mental Health' broadcast when the happiest woman in the world told us that she is a depressive, on medication, and uses exercise to combat her darknesses. I pondered deeply through the breathing exercises that followed.

Friday at 8.30 a.m. and it is the oxymoronic land-swimming class on Zoom. Phone against a cushion on the floor this time to make sure the impossibly flexible Augusto can complement me on my perfect downward-dog press-up. Another

179

oxymoronic conundrum. He only manages encouraging comments to the girls who are wearing crop tops. The boys barely get a mention. We all did very well and see you next week.

Midday Monday and fellow faster swimmer Prof Greg does a flashback Facebook High Impact session. One he used to do while getting in shape for the Olympics back in the 1980s. Sweat pumping, triceps screaming and the Prof telling me that I love it.

Oh please let me back into the pool.

Alison
Wildlife is Not in Lockdown

06 May 2020

It started with a slow-worm party. More of that later.

While we have been so busy in lockdown, trying to sort out new ways of living, organising new priorities, trying to understand how to help our families, nature has been freed from her usual state of perpetual lockdown.

Wildlife normally lives alongside us, fitting in where we allow, trying to avoid our interruptions and insensitive intrusions. In ordinary times, creatures have to lock down to survive our disturbance without us even realising.

But this is a changed world, if only for a short time. No longer is wildlife feeling the constraint of living alongside humans. No longer are species competing with us for a quiet, undisturbed space to go about their daily business of finding food, friends and shelter. No longer are plants striving to grow under the pressure of erosion from foot-fall on their particular little spot of soil. No longer are birds flying into the depths of the woods to sing their unbridled dawn chorus and evening lullabies in peace. No longer are their songs competing with the hum of urban traffic and the roar of aeroplanes. No longer are the insects of the air unknowingly breathing in particles of pollution.

No longer. The planet is resting. The planet is flourishing. Wildlife is not in lockdown.

I have seen unusual things even in my small urban Southampton environment. A woodpecker in a front garden by a normally busy main road. The clear sound of a blackbird serenading with no traffic noise to disturb. The flowers in the gardens seem more vibrant and prolific this year. The New Forest is closed – my husband works beside the Forest and is able to venture into the woods in his lunch break. It is deserted but very alive, he tells me, and that it is like some ethereal other kingdom of green, peace and lush growth, with no human competition.

Wildlife is making its own news in normally busy spots – mice dancing on a London Underground platform, a goose nesting in York station, deer grazing in a London housing estate, goats wandering down a Welsh street.

Although we are locked down and constrained, let's be glad that nature is free. It is thriving. It doesn't need us to help it thrive. It knows what to do itself. It is busy and buzzing and happy. Let us be glad, very glad, that for this short time the planet can breathe, rest, rejuvenate and excel at all it does best.

Or does it always do that every year? Maybe we have just found more time to notice? More time to see, really see; and look, really look at just how gloriously it unfolds each year?

So back to the slow-worm party. One morning I found eight under some black plastic on my allotment – I've never seen so many together. It seemed ironic that in our own isolation and lockdown, the creatures can party together more than ever before.

When lockdown ends, let's move back to our outdoor places of beauty very gently, lest we disturb the creatures that may think we have gone for good.

Ruth

Love, Death and Everything in Between

19 April 2020

My work days are generally spent in family homes, sitting on sofas, listening to the details of people's everyday lives. I learn about love, death, and everything in between. For now, these conversations are happening over the phone, and it isn't the same.

When a social worker calls our team it's because a family is in crisis. There are children that aren't safe, or their living situation isn't sustainable. Something has to change. We go out and talk to everyone in the child's network – parents, grand-parents, aunties, uncles, neighbours, teachers – anyone with a stake in that child's wellbeing. We ask what family members can do differently. Can they take over the school run, or provide week-end respite care, or maybe even have that child to live with them in the long term? We don't get called in when things are going well for a family, and for that reason the conversations we have are intense, and emotional, and detailed. We hear about trauma, abuse, addiction, mental health difficulties, illnesses, poverty . . . and the very specific dynamics of every individual family.

We talk about why professionals are worried about the child. Sometimes family members know why a social worker is involved. Often they don't and have only an idea of the extent that addiction has gripped a parent, or the full impact of their mental health crisis. They might not know that the child has disclosed abuse to a teacher or is going to school hungry every day. We listen, most importantly, to what that child wants. Are they worried about their mum because she can't get out of bed in the morning? Are they scared of Dad because he shouts and hits? What do they want to happen? That's not a conversation that works well on the phone.

We bring families together – doing whatever we need to achieve this. It might include mediation, repairing relationships, getting long lost relatives back in touch. All so they can rally round a vulnerable child.

Our days right now are the opposite to how we normally work. The enforced distance and lack of face-to-face conversations mean we can't build that rapport. We can't read body language, or offer a tissue when things get painful to talk about.

What we can do, for now, is reassure families that we are still here and ready to knock on their door as soon as we are allowed. We will be there to mobilise their family, ready to book the Church Hall for the next available Saturday morning, to buy the tea and biscuits, and to support a family in crisis.

Naomi

Infertility in a Time of Coronavirus

07 May 2020

It was the end of February and I was eager to turn the page of the calendar to mark the beginning of a new month, and what felt to me like a second entry into 2020. The past two months had been marred by fertility injections and the false hope of success that had culminated in a miscarriage. March was the month to reset and restart life in this new decade that still, I told myself, held so much promise despite our disappointment. Standing at the kitchen window looking out upon the barren border where our rabbits had played and frolicked before the night of the fox, I said to my husband that I felt that something major was about to happen in our lives. I didn't know what it was, but I knew it wasn't a baby.

By the end of the month we were in lockdown and it was time for the telephone consultation to discuss our failed cycle – by now IVF clinics had ceased all treatments so I knew that we had an uncertain wait ahead. At least we weren't in the middle of a cycle – we didn't have to postpone an egg collection or embryo transfer – so our hopes of cradling a baby in 2020 hadn't been dashed by this deadly virus that was spreading its tentacles across the globe. The consultant drew up our next and final treatment plan for the single embryo awaiting us in their deep freeze and told us to contact the clinic on day one of our next cycle. That day has come and gone, but I haven't been in touch: I don't want to be that desperate woman emailing the nursing staff asking them to look into the future and see when we may have a potential start date for our final treatment when the nation's heath is crumbling around us, and I can't help but ask myself whether it is utterly selfish to want to grow a family when so many families are mourning their lost loved ones?

There will, I hear, be a lockdown baby boom, but as it is with these things, for reasons unknown, we – and many others – will be left off the guest list. Instead, we wait, and we hope, as we cherish the time that we have with our miracle eighteen-month-old. We chronicle his time spent in lockdown, his obsession with cuddling everything that he likes, most prominently our air fryer which he affectionately calls the 'Beep Beep', and my heart rejoices as we hear his little voice as he wakes up saying, 'Cuddle Mummy, cuddle Daddy, cuddle Beep Beep,' and we smile as he asks Alexa to play his favourite songs again and again and again. Now bath times always have Daddy running the show, who has gained ten hours a week from not having to commute, and the giggling and fun that reverberates around the house silences – just momentarily – coronavirus, as our lives have been allowed to continue, and our family bond strengthened, and I wonder if there is something perverse in admitting out loud that I am enjoying lockdown, just the three of us?

I try to see the light at the end of the dark tunnel of infertility and I have come to terms with the idea that there will be no 2020 baby for us. Lockdown hasn't robbed us – like it will have many others – of the opportunity to become parents: it has given us more time to rejoice in what we already have. We can still hope that our final embryo will deliver us a sibling for little James, but if it doesn't, this time has shown us that we have all that we need in each other.

Ellie

I Am Just His Teacher

08 May 2020

I'm sitting in the sunshine in a stranger's garden. I was surprised to have been invited in and expected no more than a door-step chat at a distance.

I watch the boy investigating and exploring an enviable array of toys, bubbles and slime. He looks happy, relaxed and is more talkative than I've ever known. His hair has grown since I last saw him and I feel so glad to be with him. He laughs and plays and asks me to watch his experiment with a slide and some slime. I try to watch attentively but my attention is torn between him, the slight-framed, tousle-haired boy, and answering questions, the details of which require my consideration. His face is eagerly trying to sustain my attention and I reassure him that I see him. I clasp my mug of tea because even though it's a hot, sun-drenched day, tea is my comfort in difficult situations and when asked if I would like a cold drink, my hesitation indicated that I did not, and I was asked if I'd like tea or coffee instead. My relief showed and the mug was received with gratitude, breaking the awkwardness of strangers keeping a distance in a garden in the most difficult of circumstances.

He flits to another toy – a ribbon that dances behind him as he runs. I turn to the stranger; we have a moment to exchange hushed conversation as we eagerly share accounts of what we know and have observed and understand about the pale little boy who's wearing a smile for us today.

I anguish over his life details and I am so very sorry. I look at the stranger and reassure her of how grateful I feel. Inside I am processing everything and am impressed by her evenness and kindness. I feel increasing relief the more I hear her talk and become convinced that she's perfect. But she is realistic. She goes on to remind me that her own child must be priority. And I see how it will be. The little boy will always be someone else's child. She is of course right and I try to reason that there is little point rescuing one child only to abandon another. I feel uneasy as the tussle begins in my mind. This isn't what I want, I want someone to love him as equally as their own child. Yet I know that this will not be possible. She is after all his short-term foster carer. I have no rights and little say during this process and I've seen that he has even less.

The family's involvement with social care has been intermittently present since he was in utero. I know lockdown forced an inevitable situation and I am grateful. He was taken into police protection, bringing with him the clothes he was wearing and his teddy. He's slept and eaten voraciously since.

I've fought battles for him of which he'll not be aware – there aren't advocates for children and the process is mechanistic. It's based on the arena of the courtroom and likelihood of barristers to tear a case apart. This is what has to inform the social workers' line managers. I reflect on my way home that Local Authorities shouldn't have to pay court costs for these proceedings. I also know that the foster carer works for an agency who will likely charge three times more than local authority foster placement.

He'll also never know about the degree to which I care for him even though he cannot be part of my life. I grieve deeply for the life he had a right to but, for six years, has been denied. But I am just his teacher.

Oliver (age 11)

Lockdown Feels Like it's Going on Forever . . .

12 May 2020

The day coronavirus lockdown started was very strange. At school, the teachers tried to tell us that we may not be coming back to primary school, as we were in Year 6. Also, I had just been given the responsibility of being head boy, and it felt very strange that I may not be able to come back and fulfil those responsibilities.

At the end of the day, when we'd finished all our work and packed our bags, some people took pens out and offered their shirts to their friends and classmates to sign, which every Year 6 child does when they leave school. But my teacher said we weren't allowed to do this because she didn't want to cause anxiety for anyone who was sad to say goodbye, and there was a chance we might come back to school anyway.

When I came home everything felt different. There was an air of nervousness. I wasn't sure where we'd be able to go, who we'd be able to see – could we even leave the house? I went to bed that night with all these questions buzzing around my head.

I woke up on my first day of lockdown feeling positive. My mum left for work and my sister and I got busy doing Joe Wicks PE. After half an hour of that we did an hour of reading. We got on with our school work – our teachers had set maths, English and topic work. After completing that we went for a short walk with our dad (who was working from home) and then Mum arrived home with some surprising news. She had been told not to go back to work, and that's when I realised how extreme the situation was.

I have found it really difficult only being able to go outside for one hour a day for exercise. We used to enjoy long bike rides, visiting the beach, the park and National Trust properties. I sometimes feel claustrophobic – my mum says I have cabin fever! I have really missed being at school. At school we always have lots of different projects happening, and there's always something different to work on. I also miss my friends, mucking about on the playground and school dinners. I miss the babble and noise of the lunch hall.

Lockdown feels like it's been going on forever. Yesterday the Prime Minister announced we can exercise outdoors more, and we can travel a short distance to exercise. This information brought some joy to me, as it gave me hope that one day we will get 'back to normal'.

We are experiencing what it was like in other times of distress – such as the war and other pandemics. I hope this will have a positive effect on us all and we will be able to appreciate our freedoms more in future.

Mehri

A Morning's Work

29 April 2020

What with the pandemic, home schooling, and my grown-up daughter suffering from coronavirus symptoms, I am asked to give a hand with an art session.

I stack some books on the kitchen table and place my iPad on top and select images for discussion on my phone. I smile at my granddaughter Aara who is nine and lives five hours away. We are going to think about *Observational Drawing*, I say. Open a fresh page in your drawing pad and write this as the title with today's date. She nods attentively and proceeds. I explain that observational drawing is about looking and looking; and looking again. I ask her to write this under the title. We then look at the image of a tulip from her garden sent to me by her mummy. We speak about what we can actually see. Photographed from above we establish no stem is in view, just soil. We observe six bright yellow petals rising and opening from a sharply formed black centre. We look at her drawing. We discuss more images including David Hockney's recently released paintings of blossoms and daffodils. Thirty minutes already! We blow kisses, and Aara goes to her garden to observe and draw another tulip.

Adrian rushes into the kitchen and says, 'It's working beautifully, it's fantastic, thirty-one are attending, all these little squares, and suddenly one person moves, more like a shuffle, and a hand goes up with a question or comment . . .' He has been working on finding the best online system to hold these three-hour seminars. Seventy and never happier working; a drink of water and a piece of cheese in his mouth, he disappears down the corridor.

Time for my daily walk.

Out of the house, left and left again along the now quiet A257. It's a Roman road. Cross it and I am in the vast apple orchards, eight fields and the woods beyond. I am grateful for the Right to Roam law fought for by ordinary citizens one hundred years ago. I walk-run the gently sloped paths and near the end I hear a gentle quack-quack. I look up anticipating a flock but see two mallards circling. Undisturbed by my presence and the piercing sound of a shotgun from the farmer beyond, to disperse crows and pigeons, the mallards gracefully land. The puddles in between the rows of apple trees shine and reflect all that is around. Captivated, I note the opalescent emerald green of the head of one, and the shades of brown of the other. They are beautiful and small, never far from one another as if connected by an elastic band. With a sound of gentle munching, they feed, paddling, heads in the shallow water, walking and looking . . .

And I think to myself, 'a loaf of bread beneath the bough and thou beside me in the wilderness'?

Lydia

Freddie

08 June 2020

The family stands two metres away from me. Tears roll down their cheeks and the children hold tight to their mother's hands. 'I'm so sorry,' I say, 'but our current social distancing measures mean that only one of you can be present as Freddie passes away.' They nod their heads in understanding and their father steps forward.

Freddie slips away peacefully in his arms. I stand two metres away in a surgical mask, visor, disposable gown and gloves. The man leans over Freddie's body, buries his face in his fur and weeps. I stay my two metres away, wishing the rest of the family could be there, and wishing that I could put a hand on his shoulder. After the man has gone, I gently stroke Freddie's head, and think of his family going home to an emptier, quieter house. 'Freddie always wakes us up at 6 a.m. for his breakfast by deliberately knocking something over,' the man had said as he turned to leave.

Twenty minutes later, I laugh out loud as an eight-week-old springer spaniel puppy called Merlin wiggles in my arms and tries to lick my face. Owners cannot currently enter the practice with their animals, which means that I can spend a few minutes in my consulting room cuddling Merlin and feeling some of the sadness ebb away. Merlin loves the attention, until I give his vaccination. At which point he gives me a quick, reproachful look, turns his back on me and stares pointedly at the door. I can't blame him.

After lunch, I'm doing a video consultation with an owner who is shielding. We laugh as her cat Peanut nuzzles the screen, blocking the view of Hamish the dog who I am supposed to be examining remotely. As I hang up, the owner gives me an odd look. I realise, too late, that I did the 'funny wave' that my friends and I have perfected during our Zoom catch-ups. Fantastic.

Andrew
Alzheimer's in Lockdown

20 April 2020

Lockdown, there it is, a candidate for Word of the Year 2020.

It means many things to many people. I have, over the last five years, watched my wife of forty-nine years go slowly into the lockdown that is Alzheimer's. The beautiful person has faded before me. Once an outstanding headteacher she is a shadow now. She is in a care home being locked down in every way. Not visiting is difficult and has removed a key part of my day and we are in danger of losing the remaining bonds we have. She is receiving amazing care; I have every confidence in the staff having witnessed so many moments of kindness and tenderness willingly given to the residents in their care. It must be difficult for the staff in the home. Keeping dementia residents in their rooms as much as possible must be a challenge. My wife likes to wander and engage with people, so I wonder how she is feeling. The staff are checking temperatures regularly and wearing PPE, so how are the residents reacting to these alien arrangements? So many questions.

Think how the staff in care homes must also miss the interaction with visitors, the help these visitors provide in entertaining the residents and, where necessary, helping with care. Thank you to all the incredible care workers across the country.

The lockdown experienced by those caring for Alzheimer's sufferers is also very real, as to a large extent, your life closes down alongside your loved one. The slow withdrawal from social settings and the physical decline in your loved one shrinks your experience of life. So, what do you do when your partner goes into care? First, you feel guilty and a failure for not being able to manage at home any longer. The heartbreak associated with the decision to put someone into care can only be understood by those who face it. Then, after the tears, you make plans, play more golf, join a bowling club and then the decision whether to try to meet someone else to have a social life again raises its head. More heartache and guilt follow but in a low moment I join a dating site. All the adolescent anxieties around meeting new people re-emerge in my seventy-year-old mind. I meet someone who seems to understand the situation, it's nice, and adult conversation and a bit of banter return to my life. I am ridden with guilt but feel alive.

Then the virus intervenes, delaying the development of that relationship. This gives me endless time to reflect on what is happening in my life and whether I am doing the right thing.

Then there's finding the money to pay for care and the worry around how long it will be before I need to sell the house. Will the virus cause house prices to fall? Will the cost of care go up because of the increased challenge presented by the virus? Will Boris keep his promise to fix social care?

This virus has long tentacles and will find its way into many aspects of our lives for some time to come. Are we ready?

Karen

Phonics and Flowers – a Responder's Story

09 June 2020

It buzzed! I had been waiting for so long, I kept looking at the phone and wondered if all the settings were correct. Finally I got an alert and called the 'vulnerable' person. 'Hello, Karen here, NHS Responder, how are you doing?' An older lady replied. 'I can't stand it,' she said, 'I'm so lonely.' She started to cry. 'OK,' I told her, 'I'm coming to see you.' I jumped in my car and my husband took over the home schooling of our six-year-old – something about the American Civil War!

I was about to start the car and I suddenly thought – what am I doing? I can't go and see her. I'm not allowed. I can't sit with her and chat, give her a hug and tell her things will get better. I called her again. 'Sorry, I can't come to you but we can chat on the phone?' – which we did for over an hour. She was Spanish, and had come to London in 1975. I gathered that she wasn't particularly in need of food, or anything, she was just really sad. Towards the end of the call I asked her if she had many friends – yes, she said, I have many in Spain, but they're all underground, and then laughed . . . she had a wicked sense of humour and was giggling towards the end of the call. I hoped giving my time helped. It was rewarding for me and gave me a welcome break from phonics!

A few days later an alert took me to an old lady in a tower block in West London. Apart from the bread, milk and biscuits requested, I bought her a bunch of flowers since she had sounded so sad on the phone. Gloves and mask on, I knocked on the door and stepped back. She opened the door and burst into tears, telling me she had lost her forty-year-old son recently (not from Covid-19). She was grieving alone and looked older than her years, hunched over almost as if about to fall forward – the way someone is when they are grieving. I was lost as to what to say. I'll pray for you, I said, I'm so sorry, I said. My words felt inadequate. She kept saying over and over, you brought flowers for me. When I left, I took a photo of the view from those thirty floors up. I thought about my six-year-old boy at home and how frustrated I get when he won't sit still to do his work. I felt grateful for my son, when she had lost hers. I vowed to have more patience with home schooling.

For the next alert, amongst the twelve cans of sardines, bleach and custard, I popped in a small bunch of flowers. They seemed to bring a smile to an otherwise confused and exhausted face.

Valentina

Volcano

24 May 2020

My adult daughters, who live at home, and I could no longer cope with the strain of living on the edge of a volcano. A volcano which threatened to erupt at any time with frightening and devastating impact. My husband is that volcano. Ground down by the psychological abuse, six months ago, I consulted a divorce lawyer. The outcome was not positive. Divorce was not possible without losing half of everything I had worked so hard for and to which he had never contributed.

Then the coronavirus hit us. I was mildly ill and my sister spent three days in bed battling the illness but my husband, in his early seventies and with several health conditions, developed a high temperature. For a week he lived on paracetamol refusing to follow any other suggestions for reducing the fever. He lay flat in bed, fully clothed, covered with layers of bedclothes. No amount of persuasion would convince him to drink water; he had to have fruit juice. My daughters cared for him with endless patience despite his insults and determination not to follow advice.

The inevitable happened. He collapsed and was taken to hospital. It was a worrying time. Yes, despite everything, we were shocked and worried. It was hard to see the ambulance bearing him away. How did we all feel? My nine-year-old grandson captured it with his innocent comment, 'It is so peaceful in the house today.' It was difficult not to feel guilty when we caught ourselves enjoying our family meals, knowing that our chats were not going to trigger an outburst of abuse.

Calls from health professionals at the hospital, concerned for this 'very pleasant' old man, sounded like accusations. 'Why doesn't your husband have glasses? Why doesn't he have dentures? Why doesn't he have a mobile phone?' What could I answer? He won't go to the optician or even try reading glasses, he refuses to go to the dentist, he believes that digital technology is intrinsically malevolent (he has never even used a cash point).

My husband was lucky. He is back home albeit with even more health conditions. His behaviour, though, has not changed and we are back to tiptoeing around the edge of the volcano, worried about the possible impact of our every move.

Tilly (age 11)
How I Feel About Lockdown!

20 May 2020

I feel OK about being in lockdown except the part that we cannot go out and see our friends or go to school. This is a big thing for my year 6 friends and me. We have missed lots of school trips and activities, and our first ever residential trip, to Heatree, has been cancelled! We have not had the chance to say goodbyes or good lucks because we cannot see each other until lockdown is over. Then, hopefully, we can meet up. Lockdown is fun because you get to spend more time with the people you live with. I get more time doing no schoolwork because nearly every day we do it up until lunchtime, then enjoy some family activities and games, or go for a cycle or play outside.

My daily routine

First in my daily routine I get out of bed and I go downstairs and have some free time on the

Nintendo, iPad or my iPhone. Then, at about 8.30 a.m., we have breakfast (normally a bagel). We go back in the lounge and do ten minutes of *NumBots* and *Times Tables Rock Stars*. When this learning is finished, we go upstairs and brush our teeth, brush our hair, get dressed, make our bed, turn off our lights and open our curtains. And that is the start to my morning routine.

Different celebrations

First, we celebrated Easter. My mum and dad made an Easter hunt for my sister and me and at the end was an Easter egg and a stuffed animal (a bunny rabbit) each, and we also had a nice surprise lunch. Next was VE Day 75, for which we made a lot of drawings and banners that we hung up on the outside of our house. We also had an amazing lunch.

After that it was my eleventh birthday. I got a lot of nice presents from my family and friends, many delivered through the post. My birthday was Hawaii themed, so I dressed up as a hula girl. I played a lot of party games like a llama pinata, pass the parcel, lucky dip and limbo. I had an amazing birthday thanks to my wonderful family.

Arts and crafts

While we've been stuck at home, I have done lots of different crafts such as drawing competitions for my school, painting rainbow pictures to display in our windows to show thanks to keyworkers and the NHS, and lots of baking and cooking. I have also made a fairy garden, a bird box and a lettuce garden, and I've dug a pond.

I have also had to do six activities to earn a very special Mayflower 400 badge for my Girl Guides division.

Nathan

I Want to Start My Life

07 May 2020

I'm eighteen years old, and I'm one of quite a few transgender people living in the UK. I came out to my friends over a year ago now, but I haven't been able to tell my parents – my family aren't really accepting of trans people, and it took them a long time to come to terms with the fact I liked girls. I was planning to go to uni this September, after finishing my A-levels, and encompassed in that journey was beginning my physical transition and breaking free from the person I have been before. With time away from my parents I thought I would finally have a chance to come to terms with my life and where I want to go from here. Well, the pandemic has put an end to that.

Where I was usually going out and presenting male at school, at home I now have to pretend I'm somebody else. I haven't been called my preferred name in a long, long time but it's still hard readjusting to what I used to be called. Not only this, but before the pandemic hit there were a few things to aid my transition that I had been planning to order. But now my family is making us disinfect the post, it's kind of hard to hide what's coming in and out of the house. I'm endlessly frustrated that I can't leave the house and take on the identity I feel that is really mine, and a constant worry is that I'll slip up, or not be able to hold it in any longer. Spending all this time with my family and holding it in while they call me 'a pretty girl' and such well-intentioned things is like torture.

I trimmed my hair myself the other day. It was getting long and I thought, well, everyone's doing impulsive lockdown haircuts, right? My dad wasn't best pleased. He's been begging me to grow it out for months now. I know it's my body and my life but at the same time, we're so close and I don't want to let him down.

I just want to get this over and done with and rediscover the places that accept me outside the confining walls of my home. I want to see the friends who know me as Nathan and not as something just handed to me almost two decades ago without consultation. I want to start my life.

Nicola
Married, Just . . .

04 May 2020

It's been a very special weekend – memorable, beautiful and joyful, even while vastly different to what we'd expected.

Our son and his beautiful fiancée married yesterday. Masterfully executed on Zoom with gorgeous weather, bride walking up the aisle of the perfect back garden at their new home.

It's been a long road. Spending a year planning a beautiful spring wedding. An outbreak, far away. Plans and excitement growing. An epidemic, spreading. The date is nearly here. The pandemic hits.

Expectations shrink. Most of my husband's family live abroad. They won't make it. Can I, a doctor, safely attend? Restrictions come, first no more than five people. Then no weddings at all.

Do we delay? For how long? They can't meet or touch. The bride needs to leave her accommodation.

216

Does she move into their new house in a separate bedroom? Find somewhere else? They're feeling the strain, it's getting harder and harder. Maybe a virtual wedding? What counts as marriage? We talk and we pray. As we decide that we could support, even treasure, a virtual wedding, their church pulls out, unable to commit to holding it.

Could they marry? Alone, away from their church, without legal confirmation while we watch over computer screens nearly ninety miles away?

Yes. We will wholeheartedly support them, whatever they choose.

They married, together with us and 200 family and friends, some who'd never expected to be able to make it, and elders from their church joining us. Guests share photos of their finery, their cakes and their bubbly. The sermon is preached, the prayers are said, the vows are made, and we watch, laughing, as an overexcited groom kisses the bride before he's told to. Personal songs (a family tradition) are stitched together from across the continent. We're not distant, but invited in, drawn close to share this moment with them.

We meet up afterwards, some of their closest family and friends. I see them laughing and cycling on their wedding present tandem (complete with 'Just Married' sign and tin cans), and I know that we – that they – made the right decision.

All of this, and it's hard to believe we get more. A legal wedding to follow, as soon as allowed, and, at some point, a party with dancing, Grandma's beautiful cake and another outing for the wedding dress.

I look back at the day and I know that despite the pain and the sadness that surrounds us, our families have such reason to rejoice, with a day that was so different to what we expected, yet so much more beautiful than we ever hoped. We are blessed indeed.

Karl

A Different Time

03 July 2020

Woke up. It's Wednesday. I think it's Wednesday.
Based on the belief that yesterday was Tuesday.
Yesterday I had the constant sense of unease that
it was Friday. Not that a weekend is in any way
different from a weekday; no work, no travel, no
going to the shops. Because of Covid-19 a visit
to the supermarket is quicker if I choose a non-
peak time. But peak time is now before most
people would normally shop. It's quieter if I go
when it used to be busy. Everything is so upside
down now. So: back to the present. Is it Wednesday? I get out of bed. I'm naked. I live alone
and none of my windows allows the casual outside gaze. I patter about the kitchen trying to
remember why I thought this was a good place
to solve the riddle but can't remember why I
chose the kitchen. I find myself looking at the
central heating boiler. Why? I look at the timer.

It says Thursday. Thursday 09:15. What happened to Wednesday? One riddle solved; I know why I'm standing in the kitchen but am even more confused about what day it is. Lockdown. Lockdown is opening a cupboard and ninety Bank Holidays tumble out. Each the same as the next. Each as shapeless as a stumble in the dark. At one point I decided that every day will be a Friday from now on. Why not? What difference? 'Oh, it's Friday again. That's good.' You choose. You can even do that with time. Get up when you like. Go to bed when you like. Make a day as short as you like. Turn time on its head. When my ex-wife was about to give birth to our second child the hospital kindly allowed us the use of a small private room to wait in. Our daughter was imminent, waters had broken, dilation had started then stopped. Time stood still. The arrival of a new life on pause. As we waited, deep in silence, my eye was drawn to a dinnerplate-sized electric clock set above the door. We had been allowed the room because builders had just completed refurbishment work. In reinstating all the room's functions the electric wiring of the clock had been transposed. Wired incorrectly.

Positive became negative and so the clock was now running backwards. The red second hand racing into the past. As our daughter's future was about to begin our present was hurtling backwards. But actual time wasn't. The spacing of event. Events can only move forward. Our daughter will be born. Her life will develop. Our marriage will end. The clock will get fixed. Time will move on. Covid-19 will arrive and all certainties will run backwards into event. Reality is not the division of the moment into manageable sections; it's the game to which we are all spectators. Covid-19 has taught us that we are not mightier than a microscopic virus. That's the day. That's the time. But perhaps a different time now.

Penny
Goodbye Old Friend

04 May 2020

Took my first Covid-19 funeral service yesterday. Twenty-four years a priest but no experience like it before. The large, airy crematorium usually full of people, of life, now empty and forbidding with its small number of widely spaced chairs.

I led the coffin down the aisle and once the gentlemen had withdrawn I stood at the lectern and looked out over the barrier created to separate me from the risk of infection.

The mourners, five men in black, one of whom my husband, for this was the funeral of a friend, were dotted at safe distances around the chapel. Instead of being reassuring – I knew every one of them – this looked sinister, like something from an old Cold War film. An impression given greater credence by the presence of the unblinking eye of the live streaming camera. Was I on trial here, had I done something wrong, did I have to perform in some way? My anxiety began to rise; I battled to smother it. Hadn't I done this hundreds of times before? It would be fine, just different. I opened my mouth to speak but the acoustics were all wrong! With so few people to absorb the sound we were in an echo chamber and I had to adapt accordingly. Comfort came with the singing of the first hymn, music as always with its ability to lift the spirit and summon courage. I breathed a sigh of relief, fine, just different. We said goodbye to our friend.

Something inside me rages against this situation, rages that I must timidly hide away exercising my ministry by phone, by Zoom, behind barriers. The vocation of a priest is a risky one, following where you are called, outwardly insecure, even sometimes in danger. Willing to be personally at risk in order to be of service to others. Coronavirus hugely compromises this and I rage against it. I want to be where I am most fully alive, where I am most useful, with others – but I cannot be. Even disregarding my own safety, I cannot take the chance that I might bring illness to others.

So I do the only thing I can do. I submit, I accept, I observe, I learn what I can of myself, of others, and I wait to see what treasures these strange times may eventually reveal.

Julie
This Storm Will Pass

30 April 2020

I was one of only ten allotted mourners attending my sister's funeral a few weeks ago. Due to lockdown restrictions our family had no opportunity to take comfort in the usual rituals and behaviours that can calm and soothe. I will always remember hearing the social distanced pain of loved ones that day.

My sister, Vicky, had battled serious illness for five weeks in the Intensive Care Unit of our local hospital, before being transferred to a ward where she died two weeks later. I walked out of the hospital on the night she slipped away with feelings of grief and loss, added to, in the coming days, by an immense sense of gratitude and respect for the skill, humanity and kindness of the many members of staff.

Lockdown happened around this time, and in attempting to create a sustainable routine, I began to walk daily along the canal, located just a few minutes from my home. It is on these walks taken for fresh air and exercise that I have found so much more.

Sharing the space safely with others has sometimes been challenging, and the occasional scowl from a fellow walker, and sometimes one from me, a reminder of feelings of present fear and anxiety.

Yet there have been so many lovely smiles and greetings from others along the way, and I imagine they are also grateful for the daily freedom still available to us, of being out in the world enjoying movement and fresh air. This has brought home to me how easy it has been in the past to take these freedoms for granted, and how incredibly fragile they really are.

Memories of walks here years ago with my husband carrying our beloved son on his shoulders, and of a sunny summer afternoon sitting with a friend in the welcome shade of a beautiful tree, giggling delightedly as we exchanged secrets, are lovely reminders of happier times.

Pre-lockdown walks with friends seem a sadly distant memory and completely out of reach.

Calls, texts and video calls with family, friends and colleagues have become a sometimes necessary but incredibly important replacement for being with others.

On my walks I have noticed the impossibly intense shades of blue and green plumage of mallard ducks on a sunny day, their quacks sounding more mocking than usual (do they know something we don't?). Maybe they are enjoying the respite from our bad behaviour?

The diamonds of light on the river as the sun catches the movement of water, a cool breeze on my skin, swans using the canal as a runway, their wings squeaking as they take off, and on landing, pushing their feet into the water at intervals to reduce speed, like the landing flaps on the wings of a plane. The jumbo jets of the avian world.

Along the towpath, the felling of a tree due to wind damage has created a natural bird table and is a place where thoughtful travellers have left seeds, attractive to robins, sparrows and many more. They seem to take their turn to eat without rancour. Oh dear, yet another comparison with questionable human activity.

In all these things I realise that in the grief and pain of present times, the wonders of the world are still there, to comfort, enthuse and bring solace, offering us a reminder that this storm will pass.

Clare
Letter from New Zealand

01 May 2020

I am a UK citizen and I moved over to New Zealand some twenty-five years ago. I teach English here in Ashburton and we also farm. Lockdown has been a piece of cake with 300 acres to walk in, dogs and horses. We've watched what's going on in the UK with a sort of (I am ashamed to say) self-congratulatory smugness about how we are doing and aren't we glad we moved to NZ. We've applauded Jacinda's ability to lead the world and make good choices. We love that we have 'eliminated' the virus and it never got out into 'the community'.

Maybe we thought we were untouchable.

However, Covid-19 has really brought home the implications of living overseas. When my husband and I left the UK in our thirties we had everything to gain and all we could see was an adventure. We never really considered what the

229

implications could be of being so far away from home. We used to comfort ourselves and our families by reassuring them that we could be home in a day. And we actually could, and we did on one or two occasions have to make mercy dashes due to sick relatives. James lost his mum to cancer and his dad to Parkinson's. He went home. He was with his family. I was there too.

I go home every year to spend time with family. This year, because of Covid-19 I had to cancel my trip. I love spring in England. There's nowhere so green and lush – it's the best time of year. I like swimming in the rivers, hanging out in coffee shops with my parents, going slow, spending time with family. At first, I thought, oh well, I'll be able to pop back in a month or two. But then listening to the stats, the numbers of sick and dead skyrocketing, it began to dawn on me how bad things must be. My sister works for the NHS and she had been sending me grim texts for ages – full of catastrophe and doom.

Then our borders closed. I felt like I'd been not just locked down but locked in. I couldn't get a plane even if I wanted to – and I did try. Suddenly, we'd gone from living in the safest place in the world to being trapped thousands of miles from home. Makes you think. Makes you scared.

Then my father died suddenly, of a massive brain bleed. He was in his seventies and he'd had quite a few serious health knocks but always pulled through. We had begun to believe he was invincible – but he wasn't.

I have learnt the benefits of technology and the downside of not being able to hug my mum. It makes the grief seem unreal and such a lonely, awful thing. If you can't feel and touch anyone, if you can't cry with your family, if you can't actually see your dad or even his things, then how can you really believe he's gone? If you can't smell his clothes or see his empty chair, how then can it be true?

I now communicate through social media – who would've thought. My sister FaceTimed me to tell me Dad had died. I now Skype every morning with Mum. We've had a family forty-minute Zoom meeting with the vicar – all of us in our little windows, being unusually polite. The funeral will be live-streamed and the vicar will read my words and I will sit and watch.

Now, today my sister texted me that she was so sick that she thought she and Mum had Covid-19. I am here. I am powerless to help. I can't get Mum's shopping or make her a cuppa, but I can be terrified she will die, that they will put her on a ventilator and I won't get to see her.

Over here in this surreal Covid-19 world I lurch between believing Dad is alive and that it will all be okay, and finding I can't speak and just want to hide – I go to bed, I have no energy. I am safe from the virus but at what price? When will this end?

Sophie

How Long is it Since I Last Held Your Hand?

30 April 2020

Tomorrow you will be ninety-nine years old. A birthday we thought you wouldn't see as you lay dying from pneumonia in January. For days we kept vigil in your nursing-home room, staff tearfully saying their goodbyes as shifts ended. And when you turned that unexpected corner, and began to recover, how delighted they were, producing tasty little things for you to eat, knowing you have never liked the food there . . .

How long is it since I last held your hand? I postponed my last visit because of a cold, then the next day the home was in lockdown. We were relieved. You would be safe.

Yesterday I telephoned you, and we had the usual struggle. Your arthritic hands and your stubborn refusal to master technology combine to mean that the simplest of phones presents a challenge. I hear you saying 'Hello', 'I can't hear you', over and over. At first, it's funny, but then when you eventually get the phone positioned so you can hear, and I can stop shouting, you cry. You sob. You tell me how miserable you are, and that you just want it to end. I try to talk about other things. 'Did you receive the letter I sent?' – but you can't remember, and I hear you searching for it from the confines of your bed, limited with arthritis, doped up.

And then you can't hear me again, and you sob, 'I can't hear you' over and over and over again. Eventually I grab for my mobile, and continuing to say 'I am here, I can hear you' into my landline, I phone the nursing team, and explain that you are sobbing down the phone, but cannot hear me because you have the position of the phone all wrong, can someone go and correct it? The stress of staff is apparent, they are exasperated. 'We are very thin on the ground' they explain . . .

And so tomorrow we will gather below your window to sing 'Happy Birthday', and if they have enough hands, staff will move your bed to your window, and we will hope that you can see us, though your window will be too high for us to see you. We will hope that our presence lifts your spirits, as the staff will again abandon you to your loneliness, scared to spend too long in anyone's room, even the room of someone who is ninety-nine today.

Diana

Lockdown Play Partner

13 June 2020

After coronavirus, when there is a medicine for coronavirus . . . you can visit.'

This is what my two year-older granddaughter declares during our weekly video chat.

Her four-year old sister adds helpfully, 'You're old! That's why you need the medicine to visit.'

Sunday morning video chats are the highlight of my week. Today is Monday and my heart leaps with joy when you appear on my phone screen initiating the video call. I see you sitting at your kitchen table in Bristol bursting with pleasure and excitement because you have ice lollies for pudding. Even the bowl delights you, a place to rest lollies when they are too heavy or drippy. Demonstrating this you gently perform how this works laying them down and then picking them up to lick.

We chat about colourful spirals around the milky flavoured column. My commentary is a description of how tasty they look and how the bowl works perfectly. You approve, nodding.

Our video calls replace my fortnightly granny visits. Our play is evolving to suit the medium. You carry me around the house and garden showing and telling me about your favourite places. You both take turns to hold me virtually in Mummy or Daddy's phone. Our social contact times are becoming more private.

As the big sister, you show me your 'resting spot' under the duvet on the bottom bunk. I enthuse and marvel at the restfulness of this special place and comment on the snug and cosiness of being there with you.

You throw back the duvet and announce, 'We're going on a ride.'

I join in, 'Hold on!! Here we go!!'

You disappear under the covers. I gasp and whoop, imagining a trip to the funfair, a kiddie's rollercoaster ride. This delights you, and your smiling face fills my phone screen. You are totally transported and absorbed in your imaginary adventure. My running commentary on our fantasy journey strengthens our bond. You hold my gaze, your big brown eyes looking deep into mine. You confide in me that only people you love can share your resting spot.

'I love you, Granny.'

'I love you too, M—'

The video freezes and then the phone dies. No battery left. I call back a couple of times, but our play does not get reconnected. Cut short yes, but play partners keep each other in mind. I miss you already, our next play session seems like an eternity away.

Jade
Abstinent in Lockdown

06 July 2020

When I saw the headline, 'UK NEWS FLASH: UK Schools to Close This Friday, 20 March' with a six-day-old baby in my arms, feelings flooded my body; too many to identify. My beautiful six-year-old, who has not had to share me with anyone except his Dad for his whole life will be at home with us. How was I going to cope?

We started off well, completing the work set for him while balancing Grace on my breast; answering questions on a Wednesday morning of 'How do you spell "coat"?' or 'What's 8 + 6?' Watching my son complete Joe Wicks workouts and making houses out of cardboard.

However, as time went on the morale of both of us dwindled, and electronics were the only thing that were getting us through most days as the new little human needed most of my attention.

This was not how I imagined new motherhood to be, my partner working twelve-hour shifts as a key worker, me being at home twenty-four hours a day, seven days a week, with my only adult conversations on FaceTime or Zoom with friends, family or fellow people in recovery. It's hard for people to help with the kids through the screen of an iPhone while you quickly have a shower.

I have been abstinent for the last two years and ten months, a big part of that down to face-to-face meetings with fellow people in recovery. Friends have died during this pandemic as a result of their addiction, and many have relapsed. This breaks my heart, as a small part of me believes that if we weren't in this situation, maybe those people would still be alive.

When we were once welcomed by hugs, a warm coffee and identification, now, if we are fortunate enough to have modern technology and WiFi, we must seek something similar through the screen of our phones, tablets and laptops. However, it is just not the same. I can't help but think about those who are substance dependent who don't have access to the recovery community, as I know first-hand how important that connection is to stay on the right path. I think about the friends I have seen as I drive past on my way to the supermarket, looking in a world of pain and on autopilot for their next fix, and I pray for them.

There have been times where I have thought about using, when it was appealing. I would try to justify it in my mind: 'Our generation has never lived through something like this, I have a new baby and a six-year-old, it is HARD.' That is, until I leave the house and I am reminded what addiction does to people. To people I care about. I am snapped back into reality, that where I once didn't have a home or food in the cupboards – now I do. Where I couldn't stop using or obsessively thinking – now I experience moments of peace. I feel grateful that my home has been a haven during lockdown, as at one time it certainly wasn't, and I know so many people who will have spent lockdown in fear in their own home.

REUNION

Angela

Missing Strangers

01 July 2020

As we emerge from 'lockdown' our encounters with strangers can begin again. Is it only me that has missed strangers? Although during lockdown we thought first of family and friends, my desire for wider human contact and communion grew quickly. I have missed the convivial and banal courtesies with people unknown to me, the civil inattention I politely show as I go about my daily business, and they go about theirs. I have missed the crowds of busy markets, train stations and shopping malls where I make fleeting eye contact, navigate squeezed spaces and go on my way trying not to unsettle anyone. All this I have missed in lockdown.

Now casual conversations about nothing really very much are springing up again. I spent the first month of lockdown with my husband in New York where we were living temporarily for work.

While our experience of New York started normally enough, overnight it changed. Like the city's other dwellers we were confined largely to our home. Many of the city's public spaces and collective activities closed down immediately. New York's public and civic institutions, community organisations, cultural and leisure facilities, its department stores, tourist sites, bars and restaurants, and educational settings, gave up their famous dominance. People were restricted to their family homes, housing shelters and care facilities. The lockdown was enforced strongly by the state. Lockdown immediately changed the city and who came into contact with whom.

We are now back home in Glasgow, with the promise of emerging out of lockdown soon. Many of the city's spaces, inaccessible during lockdown, are slowly becoming available again. Encounters with strangers – bartenders, restaurateurs, library assistants, department-store staff and many more are once again anticipated. During lockdown mundane interactions with strangers were denied to me, forbidden, prohibited.

Cities are opening back up. Their sociability and collectivity are once again asserting themselves.

We city dwellers yearn to congregate, interact and make human contact. For many of us our default is density and proximity. Exposure to, and contact with, the city's diversity and heterogeneity is desired. We seek to get to know one another, to anticipate difference as a rich cultural and bio-graphical resource, rather than as a problem.

One of the starkest realisations of lockdown is social segregation, which denies us access to others – not only access to family friends and loved ones, but also to strangers, whose presence among us makes the city what it is. Strangeness is an opportunity for encountering difference as unique, and as a chance of expanding our horizons. I have missed strangers in lockdown, and am looking forward to running into more of them again some time soon.

Sarah
Making the Grade
07 June 2020

Determining my students' GCSE and A-level grades this year has been a weighty burden yet in some ways empowering. My teacher friends and I have often joked how liberating it would be to cut out exams altogether and simply allocate a grade for each student. Sparing our over-burdened students from wading through the heavy, unstoppable wave that is the exam season would, we used to argue, spread joy through every hot and stuffy classroom throughout the country.

But this year when the Covid-19 pandemic gave us that opportunity, the reality felt quite different. The biggest challenge has been to separate the heart from the head, the emotional response from the rational response. We have had to predict grades based entirely on the cold-hearted evidence in front of us. And that has been difficult. As teachers we invest our hearts and souls into our students. All those late nights spent marking in pyjamas; all those painful detentions pushing reluctant, hormonal teenagers up to the next grade; all that invested energy. It is all worth it because we know that in helping our students to achieve, we are helping to nudge open some doors for them, helping them to access their dreams and aspirations.

Sitting in front of a spreadsheet, typing in a grade which we know could close those doors, goes against everything we believe in. This is especially true when we know that a particular A-level grade is required for a particular university course. What right do we have to bolt those doors if we know that a hard-working student could, with luck on their side, attain that sought-after grade? Each year some students achieve grades beyond our expectations while others miss that crucial grade by just two or three marks. What right do we have to determine the winners and the losers this year?

Yet there are benefits too. The determined Year 11 student who always found Spanish difficult but who steadfastly attended revision classes every week should get her grade 5 and our outstanding linguist should get his grade 9. The hard workers will reap what they have sown. So why was there an occasional nagging doubt at the back of my mind, questioning 'what if I've got it wrong?'

I am lucky to have a team of experienced, committed teachers in my Spanish Department who have enabled these decisions to be 'our' decisions rather than 'my' decisions. Behind every grade and every ranking decision has been careful consideration, rigorously defended counter-arguments and of course, the inevitable and ubiquitous Zoom meetings. So thank you to A, H and J; your support and wisdom have – for now – turned the anxiety into a quiet calm . . . and for that, I am very grateful.

Laura

A Love for Local

05 July 2020

Unlike the old adage 'location, location, location', moving to our town was never a conscious choice for us: we bought the only house we could afford. We live in a beautiful part of the UK but our town is the local black sheep. People laughed when we moved here and friends with bigger incomes gave us pitying looks as they bought homes with views and gardens. Before coronavirus if we wanted to exercise, we would get in the car and drive, leaving the black sheep behind for somewhere prettier. Suddenly though, local was all we had, our town was our world. We began to explore.

In those first few weeks of lockdown we stayed within a mile of home, as if the proximity to our house was a comfort blanket, soothing us against the unpredictability of the world. We began to trudge up the steep road behind our house to the local nature reserve. Our fitness was measured by the number of times we stopped to catch our breath and by week three we could march up in one go. Every day we found a new path and a new view. During our walks my mum would teach my sons the names of wildflowers; red campions, foxgloves and, the boys' favourite, navelwort. As the seasons changed, the colours of the wildflowers deepened, as did our appreciation of our town.

One morning I found an Ordnance Survey map on the bookshelf and my son laid it out on the floor and pored over it, finding new places to explore. We walked the built-up streets of our town and the countryside that surrounds it, found holy wells and memorial plaques to battles fought long ago. We often got lost and in doing so uncovered hidden gems. When travel restrictions eased, we chose to stay local. As people flocked to the beaches, we walked to a river we had discovered, picnicking on its gravel beach and swimming in solitude.

But lockdown hasn't just opened our eyes to the natural beauty of the town, for the community spirit and generosity of local people has been impossible to miss. Ours is a town that struggles with deprivation and reputation but it is a town with a huge heart, a diamond in the rough. When the pandemic is over, should I hear anyone be disparaging about this town, I will smile to myself, safe in the knowledge that they don't know what they're missing.

Lynsey

Are You Robust Enough for this Disease?

12 June 2020

You were born just after lockdown started. Twelve weeks early and so small. 29 March ended with a late-night ambulance dash to a new hospital, roaring down a strangely empty motorway.

You always would have been locked down, coming as early as you did. So small – 1 lb 10 oz, or 735 g – in your incubator, your bubble to keep the warmth in. The lockdown has been a second bubble to keep the disease at bay. Ten weeks now of not seeing friends or family, not even your brother; not seeing our faces except behind a mask; not feeling touch except through gloves. For nineteen excruciating days you didn't even see us, as twice your brother had a fever so we had to quarantine. The first time, as I cried through the night, I told myself that you won't remember. The second time, we went to A&E

and were instead swabbed so that we could get back to you. I feel like we risked one child's health to see the other. Am I a bad mother?

We've all been learning a new language during this pandemic – R rates and social distancing. But we've also been learning the language of NICU and the machines around you that bubble and beep. Our new normal includes hand washing and masks, but also blood transfusions, your heart slowing down and heart echoes. Stories about a lack of PPE on the news take on a new significance when it's the nurses around you that are in boiler suits rather than gowns. When you see the testing going on again as they've run out of masks.

The nurses are our lockdown companions. We talk about lockdown and children returning to school, how crowded it is in ICU and what's going on in America. The blessing of being here is the varied company we know others lack. We've watched the regulations come in and change over ten weeks and the confusion and frustration that it's caused. The hospital, which was silent with the disease, is now waking up. But babies are still born early to this world, whatever happens outside, and so it ticks on here, just closed to visitors.

You've changed, too. Growing steadily, the monitors beeping, falling silent and slowly disappearing. You are ten weeks old and you've had more Covid-19 tests than anyone I know. As our time starts to come to an end and the world opens up, there are new worries: are you robust enough for this disease? How do we keep you safe? How long can we keep you in a bubble?

Wesley

An Empty Stadium

09 June 2020

For many, the return of live football is a gift from heaven. For me, it breaks my heart.

Brentford are my team. Not because I've lived there. But because they're my dad's team. It's a family thing. For thirty-five years I've been going to Griffin Park, a small, old and glorious football stadium wedged in between the M4 and rows of terraced houses. As the planes fly a couple of hundred feet overhead on their final approach to Heathrow, I feel happy. The only other place I've had a longer relationship with is my parents' home – our family home.

Next season we will move to a new ground. It's just up the road and it's fantastic. The club have done a great job in keeping us local and modernising without losing our soul. But it's not Griffin Park.

Before lockdown I had tickets for three more games. Time to say goodbye to the terraces I'd stood on and seats I'd had all around the ground; to remember the smell of the pies; to taste the beer in the pubs on each corner; to memorialise my home in all my senses.

That's now not going to happen.

Family is a word that keeps coming up when I think about Brentford. My dad. My siblings. My children. Family connections. And the club staff are like family too. I trust them to get some form of goodbye to Griffin Park right. I'm sure there will be a community day where we can all do our best to remember this great old ground.

If that's how the season had ended, I would have been fine with it. I'm not sure everyone would have. For me, though, that would be fine.

But now the season is going to start up again. And that means I'm going to watch the final five home games on TV. Games played in an empty, silent, desolate Griffin Park. That's not how I want my second home to go out. Those memories of the stands rocking under the weight of joy; of charging onto the pitch at promotion; of, at times, desperation and sadness and anger. But never of emptiness.

Supporting a club is a lifetime of emotional connection. The sense of place Griffin Park has far outweighs the small ground's footprint. I cannot bear to see its last game being one without people. The club is people. It is family. The league will finish – we might even get promoted. But I will feel saddened by that people-less conclusion.

Marcus

My Unexpected Second Paternity Leave

04 May 2020

Although this pandemic has sadly taken away so many and so much from all of us, as an eternal optimist I'd like to acknowledge what it's given us. For those like me lucky enough to have been furloughed from work while we're locked down at home, one gift has been the precious gift of time. But although I'd love to say I have used these weeks of lockdown to catch up on all those things I've been meaning to get round to, I'm sure that other parents will agree that it's hard to be productive when you don't have that luxury of time to yourself. I have a fifteen-month-old toddler and a wife who's working from home. So forget all aspirations of writing up my travel diaries, of reading all those books gathering dust on the shelf, of playing guitar, baking bread, drawing, home improving, meditating, composing, getting back in touch with myself and, dare I say it, actually relaxing.

Because instead I've been far too busy getting on with my new and all-consuming preoccupation: enjoying the wonderful gift of finally being able to hang out with my son, full time, all day and (more often than not) all through the night as well. It's been like having a little life coach by my side in these dark times, getting me up at 5 a.m. so that we can watch the sunrise together, forcing me out of my pjs and into the park to watch the tadpoles growing into frogs, burning off my lockdown calories by marching me up and down the stairs on his imaginary adventures. My son has helped me develop so many new skills, like teaching me how to teach him to ride a scooter or patiently helping me learn how to decipher his own invented sign language. And by gleefully ignoring my attempts to enforce social-distancing rules on our daily walk, he's brought me closer to so many new toddler friends and their parents.

Most importantly though, by taking up all my spare time he's saved me from wasting it. Wasting time on mindless Netflix bingeing, wasting time pointlessly following people I have no real connection with on social media, wasting time overindulging on booze or chocolate, wasting time nursing that self-destructive feeling of hopelessness that a global meltdown can bring out in even the most optimistic among us.

So I want to say a big thank you to you, my son, for actually making life in lockdown incredibly productive for me. Instead of reading Hesse or Hemingway we've read *The Hungry Caterpillar* . . . about a million times, to rave reviews from my ecstatic one-man audience. Instead of learning to play the Beatles back catalogue, we've learned to play our pots and pans. Instead of baking bread we've baked, and burned, and re-baked, a hundred banana oat biscuits. Instead of getting back in touch with myself I've been getting better at staying in touch with our family and friends. Instead of drawing up our family tree we've been drawing rainbows. And instead of writing up those travel journals, you've inspired me to write this.

So although I realise that this is a tough time for many, and there are bound to be turbulent times ahead for us all, my son has made me remember that life isn't about waiting for the storm to pass; it's about learning how to dance in the rain. We can't avoid this pandemic or wish it away, no matter how hard we try. So we might as well embrace it and try to gain something, anything, positive from this unfortunate turn of events. Every cloud has a silver lining, after all. Mine has been an unexpected second paternity leave. I hope you can find your silver lining too.

Judy

The Adventurer

01 May 2020

My mother Betty was ninety in January. She lives in a bungalow in Cornwall, on her own since my father died a few years ago.

When lockdown happened, she wasn't at home; she was returning from a holiday playing bridge, travelling alone by rail from Torquay. She's laughed since that she was safe because there was no one else on the train.

At home she found an old mask she'd last used when she worked as a midwife. Equipped with this and driving gloves, she sneaked into the local shop at 7 a.m. and bought her Saturday newspaper as usual. She refuses to let her young neighbour shop for her, as she is pregnant and Mum doesn't want *her* to be at risk.

She chuckled at the idea she could be recalled for midwifery duty thirty years on, and said she thought she could probably still do it.

She found some old packets of seeds and took up the black plastic she'd laid in the greenhouse to start growing tomatoes again. When she had a surplus of seedlings, she arranged a secret rendezvous with a friend in the woods to hand over the goods – maintaining social distancing of course.

She took out her bike for her daily exercise and found, to her delight, paths she hadn't known were there. She told us how it reminded her of the war as a child, when she could cycle the roads with no fear of traffic.

She recently overcame mistrust of her tablet and learnt to Skype so she could see her first great-grandchild, just a few weeks old. At first she kept the camera turned off, because of her wrinkles, but she found she could make the baby laugh by making faces at the screen.

She's always been an adventurer. She never sees the barriers, just the opportunities. My Covid-19 chronicle is dedicated to my mother and all those active ninety-year-olds waiting to come out again.

Mum, stay safe, stay home, but stay you!

Peter
Memories of Liverpool
04 May 2020

I grew up in a terraced house on a council estate in Liverpool. Virtually all the houses up and down our road had kids around the same age as my brother, sister and me. The fences between back gardens were low: how else would your mum and dad chat to the neighbours? And us kids didn't have to bother walking round the front to see what was going on next door: if there was a football flying up in the air three doors down, you could see it and, within minutes, join in!

Sundays at this time of year were magical: everyone was at home and the slightest hint of good weather brought them out into their back gardens. The noise of shears and the rhythmic whirr, click-click, click of mowers was the background to the melody of kids playing, fighting and laughing, and dogs barking. The burble of life was constant from breakfast till dinnertime – then a bit of a lull – then full blast again till teatime. Bedtime was a bittersweet experience: the kids we weren't allowed to play with were still having fun in their gardens, while we were being told to go to sleep. Later, when even the naughty kids had been wrestled indoors, we lay and listened to the blackbirds and the thrushes whistling their goodnight songs. As night eased in, the headlights of an occasional car on the main road lit up our ceiling in swooping shafts.

Since then, the cars have taken over, the fences between the gardens have got higher and Sundays aren't too different from all the other days: when there are bargains to be had at Ikea, and when you can fly to Barcelona for fifty quid for a long weekend, then why on *earth* would you stay at home? The chat over the back-garden fence has ended. The outside world has been shut out. Piercing a neighbour's bubble by communicating over the fence is against all the rules: their privacy is sacrosanct. Except that now, it isn't. There's suddenly a lot to talk about.

The sunny days of lockdown are like back-to-back childhood Sundays again. The cars are gathering the dust that comes before warm rain and even the boy racers seem to have noticed that there's no-one about to admire the size of their exhausts. The birds have recovered their voices. And over the fences comes Liverpool in 1971: the chatter of neighbours over fences that *now* seem too high and too solid, the laughter and shouting and screaming of children from doors away. The bubbling of humanity at its most appealing and vulnerable best.

Jenni

At Least

06 June 2020

At least my diagnosis came long before this crisis.

At least I wasn't put off going to the GP.

At least I was living in the UK, where treatment was available on the NHS.

At least I am young and otherwise fit and healthy.

At least I responded well to chemotherapy.

At least my stem cell transplant wasn't postponed due to coronavirus on the horizon (it was too urgent).

At least my donor was my sister, not a stranger whose donation would have needed to cross borders while the world was locking down.

At least my sister was able to come and see me receiving her cells; the same day the World Health Organisation declared a global pandemic.

At least when visitors were banned from the hospital, I still had FaceTime.

At least they were able to feed me through a tube when the side effects of radiotherapy meant I could no longer eat.

At least when my husband dropped off clothes for me, he was able to wave from across the Euston Road, thirteen floors below, while we spoke on the phone.

At least I got through my weeks in hospital without any serious infections. At least I didn't catch Covid-19 while I was there.

At least I was discharged after only twenty-six days; not the six weeks for which I'd been told to prepare.

At least my 'first hundred days' after the transplant has coincided with the twelve weeks of shielding. I'd already cancelled all my plans.

At least the world decided to put everything online, so I could join in with things I otherwise would have missed out on during my convalescence.

At least I had somebody to come home to, and to be with during the lockdown.

At least he is able to work from home while shielding to protect me.

At least – unlike him – I am allowed to leave the flat once a week for my hospital check-up.

At least I'm starting to feel stronger. My new cells are doing their job, and I'm in remission from the leukaemia, for now.

At least I won't be on this immune suppression forever.

At least in a year, I'll be able to have my vaccinations again.

At least in the meantime, I have a roof over my head, food on my plate and loved ones only a video call away.

At least I am still here.

Mary

From Ghana to Birmingham

13 June 2020

A lot has happened these past Covid-19 months. After my arrival back in Britain you see me now sitting in my Birmingham kitchen sewing face-masks from Ghanaian batik for my younger daughter and her partner who live in New York. I have sewn a stuffed turtle for their baby son who's too little to wear a mask. The batik is the same material that I tied to my anonymous black suitcases when I took the 'rescue' flight from Accra, Ghana to London. I was seeking the safest place and every day I question if I made the right choice.

The flight from Accra was grim; no food or small screen to distract us from the strangeness of it all. I came with my elder daughter and her two children. My normally carefree girl daubed sanitiser on her seats and tray tables at least five times during the night flight. We were so relieved when

272

her baby slept and stopped her innocent investigations. The flight attendants remained insulated in the galley.

We arrived at Stansted on a cold grey March morning. The airport was closed to all but the evacuated and, having come from 30 degrees heat, we shivered in the gloom.

I came without my husband. He wanted to stay in Ghana, so did, and there was no time to persuade him to cut short his holiday. Ghana then had very few cases and, after all, he had paid for his ticket to this long-awaited trip to his homeland.

We talked on WhatsApp every day and I would see his kente facemask idling around his neck and entreat him to stay safe.

Two weeks after my return to Britain, my husband's brother died. In Ghana, churches as well as borders were closed so my husband and a small group of family mourners had to go straight to the cemetery. He told me a few days later that all the mortuaries had been full so he had had to drive a further sixty miles out of Accra to find a place for his brother to lie. This shortage, he explained, is because families are saving up the bodies of their deceased relatives until restrictions are eased and they can be given a 'proper' funeral.

The first Thursday in Birmingham, we stood on our doorstep and clapped for the NHS. Actually, I shook a cabasa and my grandson banged a goatskin drum. My daughter asked me why I was crying and, at the time, I couldn't say. But I just thought how wonderful it is to live somewhere that the very fabric of the place is made to keep you safe. My husband worked as a psychiatric nurse for forty years, recruited from Ghana in 1971 and ending up in Birmingham's biggest psychiatric unit; the NHS is in our hearts. I just hope he will come home soon. The British rescue flights have rescued all that want to be, so now we wait for Covid-19 to ease its grip and let my family piece itself together again.

Valerie

Going Grombre (with style)

22 June 2020

My hair costs me £600 a year. I know this because, since lockdown, I've missed three hair appointments, saving myself £150.

Thing is, my hairdresser, Ray, has been tinting my hair to a shade approximating my schoolgirl blonde for the past fifteen years. Thereby re-establishing the 'real' me: mousey blonde with sun-bleached tendrils. This is the 'me' I've clung to up to my sixth decade.

Ray's five-weekly restoration of schoolgirl me is so effective that I've only caught occasional glimpses of my shameful grey roots. To me, grey has always reeked of old, conjuring up pictures of my mother with patches of wiry white and steel curls, crumpled face and mis-applied pink lipstick.

After the first cancelled hair appointment during lockdown, I attempted to maintain blonde me by the application of a gold powder that promised to 'banish all grey'. At a centimetre's re-growth, it did kind of work, although it was a little too . . . gold, giving me the appearance of a bust of some long-deceased queen. Plus, I could only manage my hairline. I mean, how on earth could I apply it to the back of my head?

Three months into lockdown and the grey is creeping so far down the length of my hair that my crowning glory resembles a failed tie-dye experiment. But when I take a closer look at my grey hairs, lying as sleek and flat as strands of fine metal, they're a harmonious blend of white, silver and gunmetal. Unlike the dull blonde, the grey hairs have the lambent glow of rain on glass.

The beauty of my natural grey hair begins to feel 'right', and freeing, as if I'm shedding a raw, unpolished persona – an authentic, more elegant me emerging from the shackles of moody youth.

When Ray calls to arrange an appointment for July, I tell him I don't want a colour, just a cut.

'You're the third person this week who's going grombre,' he says cheerfully. As we book our appointment I feel liberated. I'm beautiful as I am.

The relief in quietly discarding the Valerie that's been bending to the wind of convention and its celebration of youth is tangible. With excitement I join the thousands of other women across the globe who've liberated their authentic grey.

Yes, Ray, I'm going grombre. The Covid-induced lockdown has forced me to let go of my negativity towards the visual signs of ageing and given me the courage to wear my grey with pride.

Christopher
Dispatches from Furlough
12 July 2020

This morning I sang 'Happy Birthday' for twenty seconds while I washed my hands with soap and water. I sang it out loud and not, as usual, in my head. I sang it out loud because today, the twelfth of July, is actually my birthday.

It's my fifty-fifth birthday and I find myself furloughed, awaiting almost certain redundancy. As a venue executive in an historic visitor attraction, I don't think there'll be a queue of employers beating down my door to offer me work. Normally I am a positive and resourceful kind of guy but right now I feel uneasy, anxious, and I have no idea in which direction to take my career.

Today marks another notable event, my first meal out in a restaurant in over four months. As I get ready to leave I realise that I haven't been dressed in anything other than a T-shirt and trackie bottoms since St Patrick's Day! I have to dredge my thinning memory to remind myself how to iron a shirt with a collar and buttons.

Furloughed, as I have been since 01 April, I have been receiving increasingly bleak and depressing weekly updates from our Chief Executive talking of 'Difficult decisions ahead' and 'Voluntary redundancies'. I dread opening these emails and feel as each week passes I am closer to the email that will end my career; it is truly terrifying and I feel completely powerless over my future.

You're never too old to learn new skills (I tell myself), old dog, new tricks etc. And indeed, in the last four months I have learnt how to take part in a Microsoft Teams Meeting as well as increasing my vocabulary; Zoom is now something other than a hit song by Fat Larry's Band and I'd never before heard the word furlough; or Covid-19 for that matter.

The rainbows have disappeared from the bay windows of East London, applause doesn't fill my street on a Thursday evening any more and the blackbird's song competes again with the police siren and the ice-cream van. Yet I feel that far from reality returning, reality is further away than it's ever felt before.

As I head out of the house, I do my new mental checklist – keys, wallet, face mask, hand sanitiser – and I am certain of one thing: I'll have the shepherd's pie for lunch.

Frances (age 9)
Missing School

13 July 2020

Even though the lockdown is easing it feels harder as I find that a lot of my friends have gone back to school. It is really irritating when I see friends who were begging to go back one day and the next day they're in their school uniform on the climbing frame. When my six-year-old brother comes back from school he tells me about all these fun things he's done that I wish I could do. Which, unfortunately, I cannot.

I almost forgot society in the time of no social gatherings and when I first met up with a friend it felt weird at first but after ten minutes I felt at ease and we talked for ages until it was time to leave. The next week I saw another friend who has a cocker spaniel and it felt almost like normality.

When I went home after seeing that first friend, I was told my teacher was planning how we could take it in turns to see her in the playground. My mum has a job in Bristol and she bought a cool electronic desk that you can move to standing height but as I use it four out of five days, you could say it's mine. Next year I will be in year 5 and studying for tests, and I'm very glad that my teaching assistant from this year will still be with me next year, and with our school dog. He's so adorable and he came to school just before lockdown.

My cousins and I have a video call where we sometimes play chess, or when my brother gets home from school we trade Pokémon cards – one of the things that has kept us busy over these times. For the first time ever I wish there were no summer holidays because it would mean I would be back at school sooner. We bought masks from a local lady and when we go out I like to go into charity shops or non-essential ones when we need something and it feels so good. Sometimes I feel like I'm the only one still on lockdown cause my mum's working, my brother's at school and my family are all back in their old routines and lives. Even my youngest cousin is with a nanny and she's under one. I just hope in September when I go back to school everything will be a little more normal.

Sharon
Wild Swimming
06 July 2020

At this gentle place the River Tweed has already passed through the Neidpath and Dookits' swimming holes, with their rocks and rapids, and has settled to a deep, slow, wide ribbon of silk that reflects rocks, trees – pine, beech, sycamore – and plants overhanging the bank. The park is enormous, wild in places, with ancient trees, who have been my friends since childhood. After storms I go, with dread, to check who has lost a limb, or worse.

There are more herons every year it seems; a sedge of herons, and it's common to see feathery Pterodactyls 'karking' and gliding their way up the river together. Or perched in the trees, hunched over like old men in grey overcoats.

Today I have decided on a different place to swim, somewhere I call the Lazy Bend. I would never swim here on a hot day; it would be impossible to find this level of peace. The park and river would be full of kids and adults, all having the best fun. On those days I know I must turn to wilder options. Perhaps, as I grow physically stronger, I will spend less time here at the Lazy Bend anyway, but for now, it suits my solitude, my need to be alone as time with friends creates overload; after four months on my own, and five years of widowhood, I feel I have taken a step back in terms of recovery from grief and depression, but at least I recognise the signs of overload and the cure. DO less, STAY quiet, COOK every day. SWIM!

I have been wild swimming for thirty days now. Getting into the water has become easier, no involuntary noises escape me any more. It still feels cold, but I am in sheer delight at the weightlessness, the freedom, and the rich feeling of water on my skin. Darting river nymphs and yellow wagtails seamlessly make room for me. Slow water, my strokes rippling outward, create small bow waves of curved reflections of sky and trees, my breathing is regular and measured, I am swimming.

The dog sits on the riverbank, watching me, worrying when I swim too far. She potters around, fishing for stones, which she lays on the riverbank for me to throw back in, much to her joy. Her head completely submerged, Frida can fish the same stone out of the river and return it to me.

Here at the Lazy Bend, I can slowly stretch out, swim gently down the river, for a long while. I could risk the back stroke here . . .

Peebles.

Scotland.

Harriet

Let's Keep Dreaming Like This

18 June 2020

You were all there, all of you, in the dream I had last night.

It really was all of you. Not just close friends and family, but every person from every category that's marked out my life: old colleagues, neighbours, the people who work in the cafe at the end of the road.

You were all there, and it was very real – the kind of dream that looks enough like reality that, for the first moments of waking, it is.

That borderland of sleep is these days littered with nearly-real dreams, haunted by memories of mundane things I never thought I'd have to remember: what it's like to push the swing in the playground; crowded mornings on the Thameslink, so close you can read each other's emails; the detail of my mum's hands pouring tea from the pot, freckles too subtle for a video call.

All of these I keep only in dreams, for now.

Last night's one was a long and a lazy dream, uninterrupted by narrative, a feeling more than a happening. There was an enormous house, bigger than any I've ever been in, but not grand – the size more for communality than indulgence. I was in a high-ceilinged room with enormous windows onto the street. People sat with me or wandered casually around or out of the open door, the breeze nudging it carelessly to and fro. People walked in and out again with a relaxed indifference that it's difficult even to imagine.

People brought tea to each other, sitting close enough to see the steam rising off an almost-stranger's mug. It felt like a party, but without purpose – without the weight of occasion, only the simple enjoyment of existing together.

You were all there, everyone I've ever met, and you came and you went, but I felt an indescribable contentment in knowing you were there. I sat back in an armchair absorbing the conversation, luxuriating in it, fresh words still warm from the speaker's mouth, not teleported through a phone or a screen.

I closed my eyes, the sunlight making mauve butterflies behind my eyelids. It's the best way to nap, I think: in a room filled with people you love, chatting quietly to one another.

So I sleep, my sleep within a sleep, listening to all your stories and your yesses and your nos and your sounds in between.

When I wake, you're gone, or perhaps I am, having left the house somewhere I can't recall.

One day we'll find our way there, together, and we'll throw open the windows and doors, and make tea for each other, all of us, words and laughter dancing freely through the air.

Until then, let's keep dreaming like this.

Acknowledgements

The publishers would like to thank BBC Radio 4's *PM* production team, Owenna Griffiths, Louisa Lewis, Tom Baker, Emma Trevelyan, Ellie Caddell and Evan Davis; and Kishan Rajani and Clara Farmer. Biggest thanks go to *PM* listeners, who shared their stories in their thousands during lockdown and made this book possible.

All the Covid Chronicles submitted to the BBC *PM* Programme have been archived at the British Library for use by researchers and members of the public. For more information see: https://www.bl.uk/ or contact: MSS@bl.uk